Welcome to We'Moon on the Wall 2027!

We are happy to present the twenty-third edition of *We'Moon on the Wall*, inspired by the original We'Moon: Gaia Rhythms for Womyn datebook that Mother Tongue Ink has published since 1981. *We'Moon on the Wall* is a simplified version of the datebook featuring full size reproductions of 12 vibrant works of art selected from the 150+ art pieces published in the datebook. Women from all over the world submit thousands of offerings of art and writing every year to We'Moon, and the wall calendar is a special harvest of those treasures. It is a wall calendar in month-at-a-glance format with Moon phases pictured for each day. We include all major planetary and lunar ingresses, and note the full and new Moons. For Holy Days, we notate the natural turning points of the seasons that are determined by the Earth's rotation around the Sun. It is remarkable how many traditional Holy Days are clustered together according to natural cycles. There is plenty of room to mark additional holidays that are important to you. See page 34 for a list of conventional holidays.

To experience the whole tapestry of multicultural womyn's art and writing, and many more astrological details, check out the We'Moon datebook. This 240-page week-at-a-glance planner includes many astrological articles, predictions for each sun sign, detailed daily planetary aspects, Holy Day features, monthly ephemerides for planets and asteroids—all surrounded by inspired verbal and visual imagery from women exploring spiritual depths and invoking hope for Earth-life.

What is We'Moon?

We'Moon is a lunar calendar, a handbook in natural rhythms and a celebration of international womyn's cultures. We'Moon is about *womyn's spirituality* (spirit'reality). We share how we live our truth, what inspires us, how we envision our reality in connection with the whole earth and all our relations. *Wemoon* means "*women*." Instead of defining ourselves in relation to men (as in wo*man* or fe*male*), we use the word *wemoon* to define ourselves by our primary relation to the natural sources of cosmic flow. We'Moon is sacred space in which to explore and celebrate the diversity of She-ness on earth. *Wemoon* means *"we of the Moon."* The Moon, whose cycles run in our blood, is the original womyn's calendar.

We show the natural cycles of the Moon, Sun, planets, and stars as they relate to Earth. By recording our own activities side by side with those of other heavenly bodies, we may notice what connection there is for us. The Earth revolves around her axis in one day; the Moon orbits around the Earth in one month (29¹/₂ days); the Earth orbits around the Sun in one year. We experience each of these cycles in the alternating rhythms of day and night, waxing and waning, summer and winter. The Earth/Moon/Sun are our inner circle of kin in the universe. We know where we are in relation to them at all times by the dance of light and shadow as they circle around one another.

Co-op America APPROVED FOR PEOPLE AND PLANET

Published by Mother Tongue Ink
U.S. toll free: 877-O WeMoon (877-693-6666)
Local/International: 541-956-6052
email: mothertongue@wemoon.ws
www.wemoon.ws

We'

Produced by The We'Moon Creatrix: Bethroot Gwynn (Special Editor), Barbara Dickinson (We'Moonager/Production Coordinator), Sequoia Watterson (Graphic Design), Sue Burns (We'Moonager/Accounts Coordinator), Ashley Marshall (Production Assistant/Promo/Sales), Susie Schmidt, Marina and Patti Whitchurch (Order Fulfillment), Musawa (Founder), EagleHawk (Proofing).

__*Astrological Data*__
Graciously provided by Rique Pottenger.

Hansol Paper **Environmental Benefits Statement:**

We'Moon 2027 is printed on Hansol paper using 60% recycled content: 50% pre-consumer waste, 50% post-consumer waste, with Solvent-free Soy and Vegetable Based inks with VOC levels below 1%.

By using recycled fibers instead of virgin fibers, we saved:
110 fully grown trees
44,156 gallons of water
30 million BTUs of energy
2,603 pounds of solid waste
7,791 pounds of greenhouse gasses

Useful Info about *We'Moon on the Wall*

Time Zones: We use Pacific Standard Time and Daylight Time for all astrological and lunar information.

The Year at a Glance Calendar can be found on the inside of the back cover.

Astrological Articles/Info: See articles on pp. 27–32 anc

Contributor Bylines: Learn about the artists and writers

Become a We'Moon Contributor! Information can be f

Ordering Information for all of our products can be fo

AF744368

Astrology Basics

Planets are like chakras in our solar system, allowing for different frequencies or types of energies to be expressed. See "Signs and Symbols at a Glance" (p. 30).

Signs: The twelve signs of the zodiac are like a mandala in the sky, marking off 30° segments in the 360° circle around the Earth. Signs show major shifts in planetary energy through the cycles.

Glyphs are the symbols used to represent planets and signs. For a handy key with brief definitions for commonly used glyphs, see "Signs and Symbols at a Glance" (p. 30).

Ingresses (→): Indicates when the Sun, Moon and planets move into new signs.

Sun Sign: The Sun enters a new sign once a month (around the 20th or so), completing the whole cycle of the zodiac in one year. The Sun sign reflects qualities of your outward shining self.

Moon Sign: The Moon changes signs approximately every 2 to 2¹/₂ days, going through all twelve signs of the zodiac every 27¹/₃ days (the sidereal month). The Moon sign reflects qualities of your core inner self.

Moon Phase: Each calendar day is marked with a graphic representation of the phase that the Moon is in.

Direct or Retrograde (D or R): These are times when a planet moves forward (D) or backward (R) through the signs of the zodiac (an optical illusion, as when a moving train passes a slower train which appears to be going backward). When a planet is in direct motion, planetary energies are more straightforward; in retrograde, planetary energies turn back in on themselves and are more involuted.

Musawa ¤ Mother Tongue Ink 2003

Cover Notes

***Star Talk** © Jakki Moore 2015*

Since time immemorial, stars were considered ancestors—guides and keepers of wisdom. Talking to the stars and passing down stories through generations was the way spiritual beliefs and customs were shared. Women's bodies are in tune with the moon, stars, cosmos and nature. We carry the ancient knowledge of the Divine Feminine. Where women gather in harmony, Mother Earth heals.

This Moon calendar is reusable—every nineteen years the moon completes a metonic cycle, returning to the same phase, sign and degree of the zodiac.

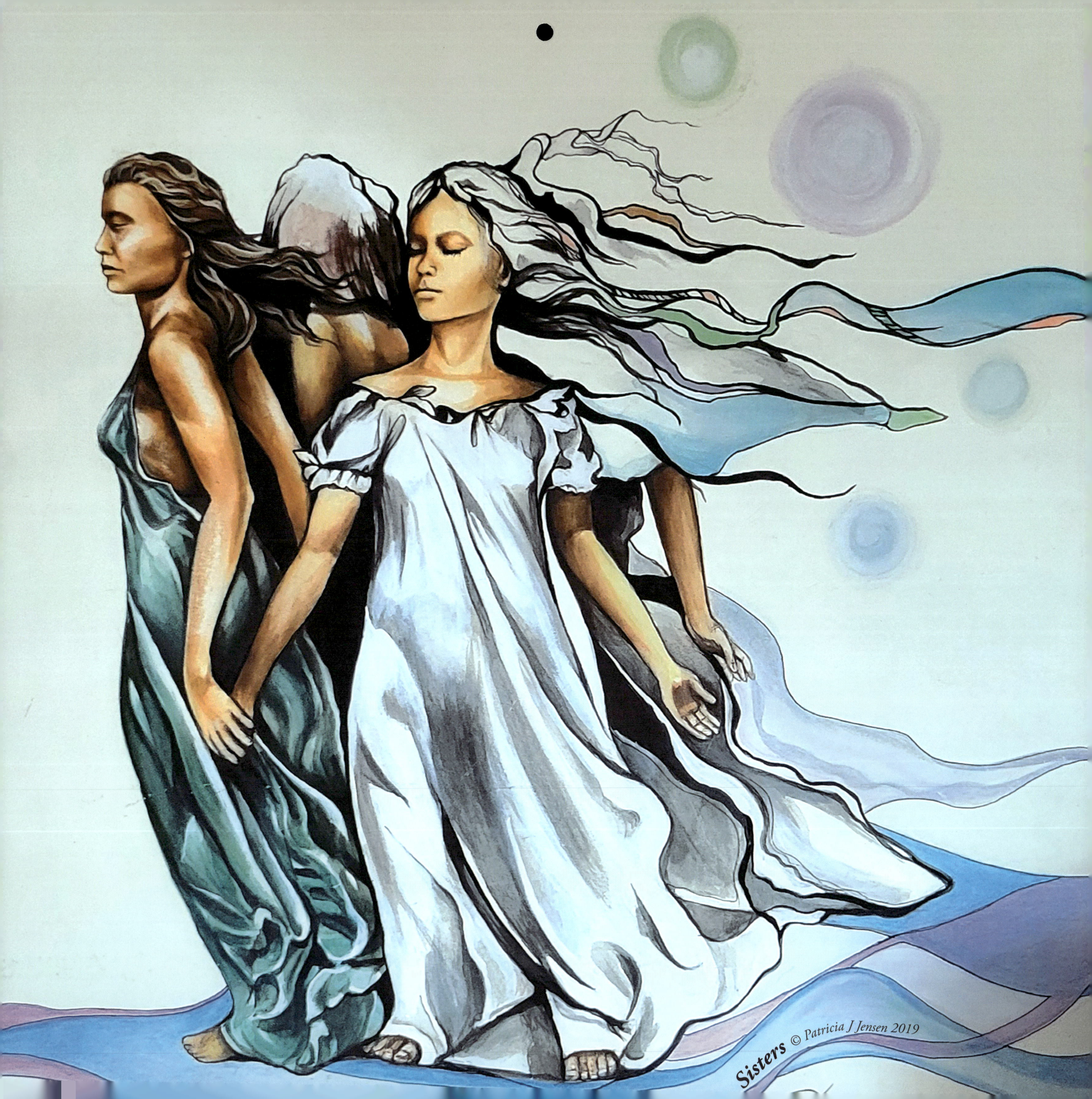

Sisters © Patricia J Jensen 2019

January

In the hush between night's last breath and morning's first yawn, a Dreambeat rises—From the Drumbeat of Time. It comes not from sleep, but from ***deep***, where the Elders dwell in the marrow of remembering.

They are the heartbeat under the ground, the voice beneath the silence, the dream that stirs before you stir.

excerpt © Andria 2025

December 2026

S	M	T	W	T	F	S
		1	2	3	4	5
6	7	8	9	10	11	12
13	14	15	16	17	18	19
20	21	22	23	24	25	26
27	28	29	30	31		

February 2027

S	M	T	W	T	F	S
	1	2	3	4	5	6
7	8	9	10	11	12	13
14	15	16	17	18	19	20
21	22	23	24	25	26	27
28						

Sunday	Monday	Tuesday	Wednesday	Thursday	Friday	Saturday
					1 ☽→♏	2
3 ☽→♐	4	5	6 ☽→♑ ⚷D	7 ♀→♐ ☉☌☽ New Moon in Capricorn	8 ☽→♒	9
10 ♂R	11 ☽→♓	12 ☿→♒	13 ☽→♈	14	15 ☉□☽ ☽→♉	16
17	18 ☽→♊	19 ☉→♒ Sun in Aquarius	20 ☽→♋	21	22 ☽→♌ ☉☍☽ Full Moon in Leo	23
24 ☽→♍ / ☿→♓ 31	25	26 ☽→♎	27	28 ☽→♏	29 ☉□☽	30 ☽→♐

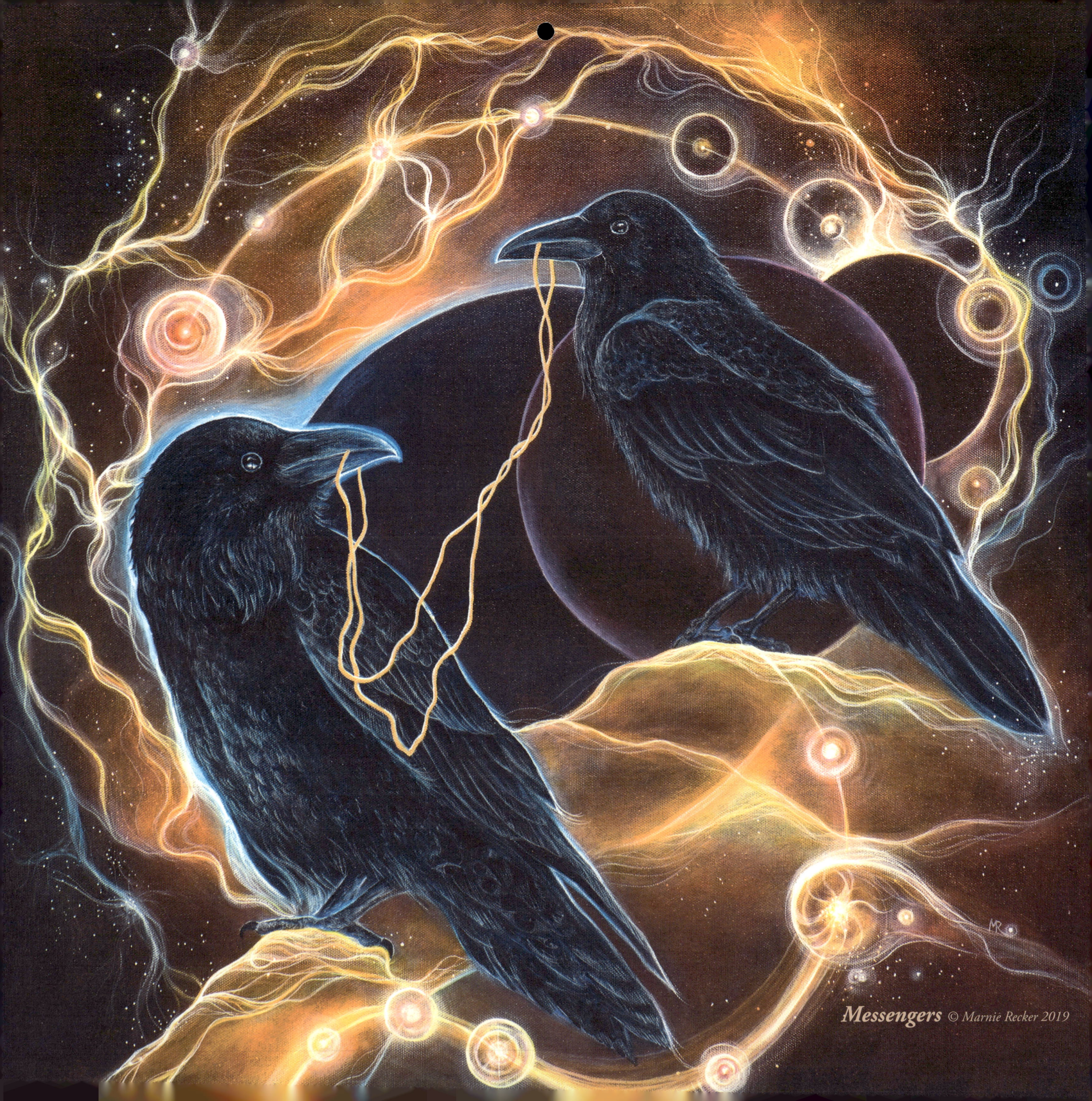
Messengers © Marnie Recker 2019
MR

February

Sunday	Monday	Tuesday	Wednesday	Thursday	Friday	Saturday
(January 2027)	1	2 ☽→♑ Imbolc	3 ♀→♑	4 ☽→♒	5	6 ☉☌☽ Lunar Imbolc New Moon in Aquarius
7 ☽→♓	8 ♅D	9 ☿R ☽→♈	10	11	12 ☽→♉	13 ☉□☽
14 ☽→♊	15	16 ☽→♋	17	18 ☿→♒ ☽→♌ ☉→♓ Sun in Pisces	19	20 ☽→♍ ☉☍☽ Full Moon in Virgo
21 ♂→♌	22 ☽→♎	23	24 ☽→♏	25	26	27 ☽→♐ ☉□☽
28 ♀→♒	(March 2027)					

January 2027

S	M	T	W	T	F	S
					1	2
3	4	5	6	7	8	9
10	11	12	13	14	15	16
17	18	19	20	21	22	23
24	25	26	27	28	29	30
31						

March 2027

S	M	T	W	T	F	S
	1	2	3	4	5	6
7	8	9	10	11	12	13
14	15	16	17	18	19	20
21	22	23	24	25	26	27
28	29	30	31			

In ancient days they read the skies.
Birds were omens
Heralding change.
These are ancient days.
We are remembering
The ways of the crow.

From north and south, east and west,
From sea and trees
From stream and field
We fly
Circling the moon,
Singing songs of silver,
In a world of tarnished gold.

Crow moon rising
Shimmering bright
A new world woven
On our wings.

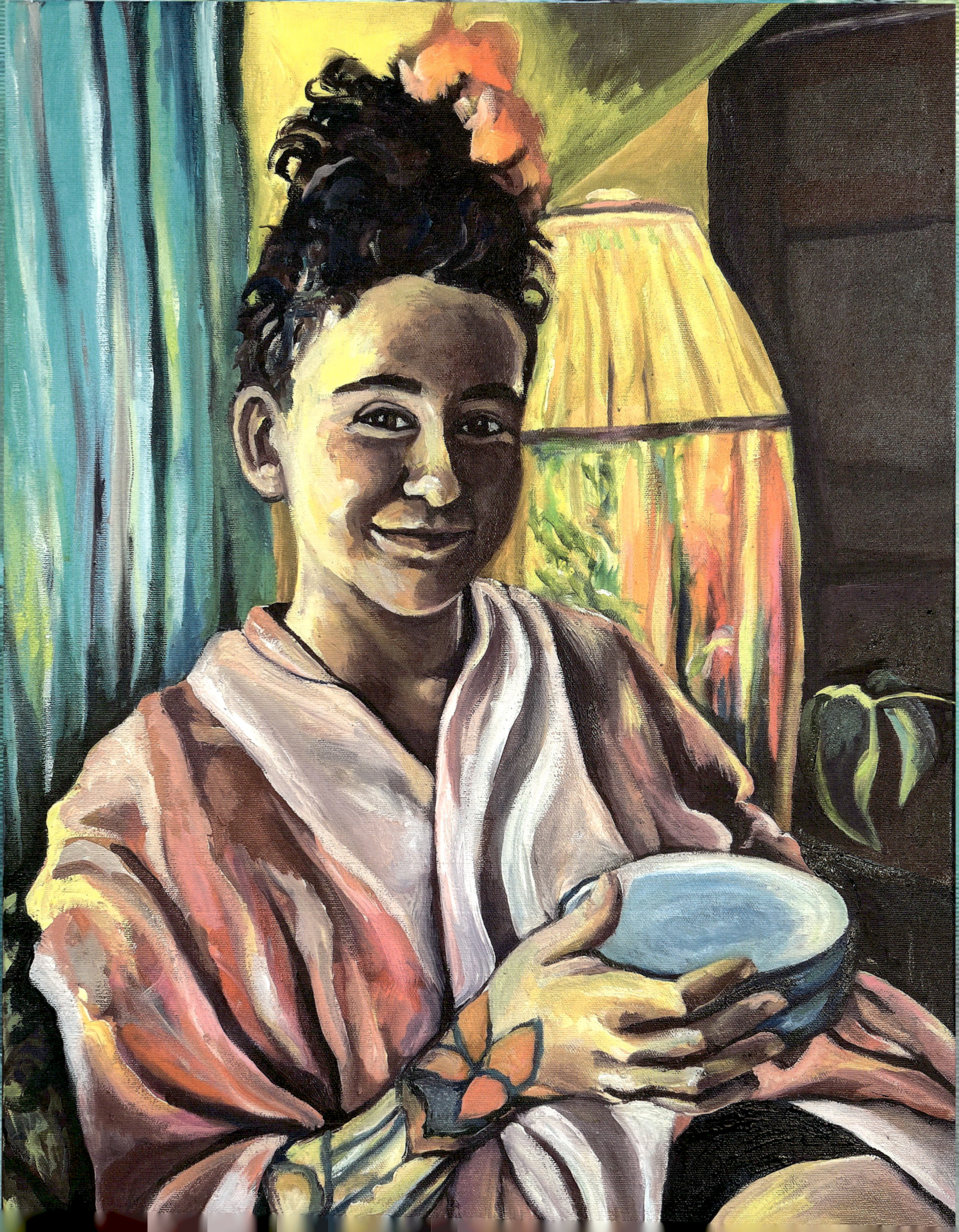

The Pink Robe *© Marla Faith 2023*

March

Sunday	Monday	Tuesday	Wednesday	Thursday	Friday	Saturday
(February 2027)	1 ☽→♑	2	3 ☿D	4 ☽→♒	5	6 ☽→♓
7 Daylight Saving Time Begins 2:00 am	8 ☉☌☽ New Moon in Pisces	9 ☽→♈	10	11 ☽→♉	12	13 ☽→♊
14	15 ☉□☽ ☽→♋	16	17 ☽→♌	18 ☿→♓	19 ☽→♍	20 ☉→♈ Spring Equinox Sun in Aries
21	22 ☽→♎ ☉☍☽ Full Moon in Libra	23	24 ☽→♏	25	26 ♀→♓ ☽→♐	27
28 ☽→♑	29 ☉□☽	30	31 ☽→♒	(April 2027)		

February 2027

S	M	T	W	T	F	S
	1	2	3	4	5	6
7	8	9	10	11	12	13
14	15	16	17	18	19	20
21	22	23	24	25	26	27
28						

April 2027

S	M	T	W	T	F	S
				1	2	3
4	5	6	7	8	9	10
11	12	13	14	15	16	17
18	19	20	21	22	23	24
25	26	27	28	29	30	

Each day holds a threshold moment
whether you know it or not.
The pause between this place and that.
An opportunity for change, a chance to break
an old pattern, or start something new.
You can choose to show up and pay attention,
to be awake for these moments.

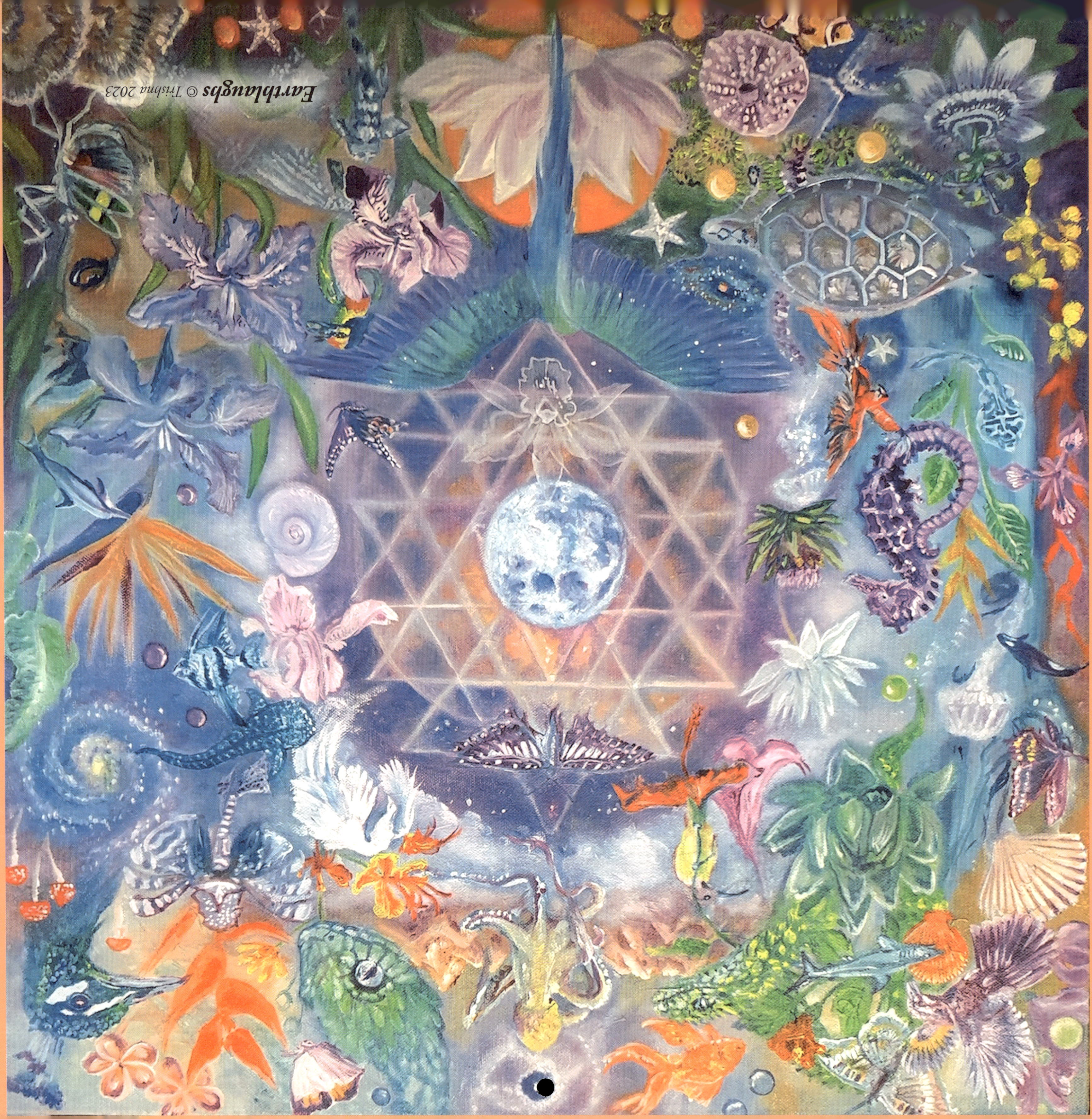
Earthlaughs © Trishna 2023

April

Winding our way through a wetland labyrinth
chants of red wing blackbirds, the plunk of fish,
a slightly seen path beckons into territory of
iridescent turquoise dragonflies
carpets of tiny succulent greens
served on reflective blue glass
where water-lilies blossom blessings
and floppy-winged herons circle slowly above.

excerpt ¤ Holly Wilkinson 2015

March 2027

S	M	T	W	T	F	S
	1	2	3	4	5	6
7	8	9	10	11	12	13
14	15	16	17	18	19	20
21	22	23	24	25	26	27
28	29	30	31			

Sunday	Monday	Tuesday	Wednesday	Thursday	Friday	Saturday
				1	2	3 ☽→♓
4	5 ☽→♈	6 ☉☌☽ New Moon in Aries	7 ☽→♉	8 ☿→♈	9 ☽→♊	10
11 ☽→♋	12 ♃D	13 ☉□☽	14 ☽→♌	15	16 ☽→♍	17
18 ☽→♎	19 ♀→♈	20 ☉→♉ ☽→♏ ☉☍☽ Lunar Beltane Sun in Taurus Full Moon in Scorpio	21	22 ☽→♐	23	24 ☿→♉
25 ☽→♑	26	27 ☽→♒	28 ☉□☽	29	30 ☽→♓	

May 2027

S	M	T	W	T	F	S
						1
2	3	4	5	6	7	8
9	10	11	12	13	14	15
16	17	18	19	20	21	22
23	24	25	26	27	28	29
30	31					

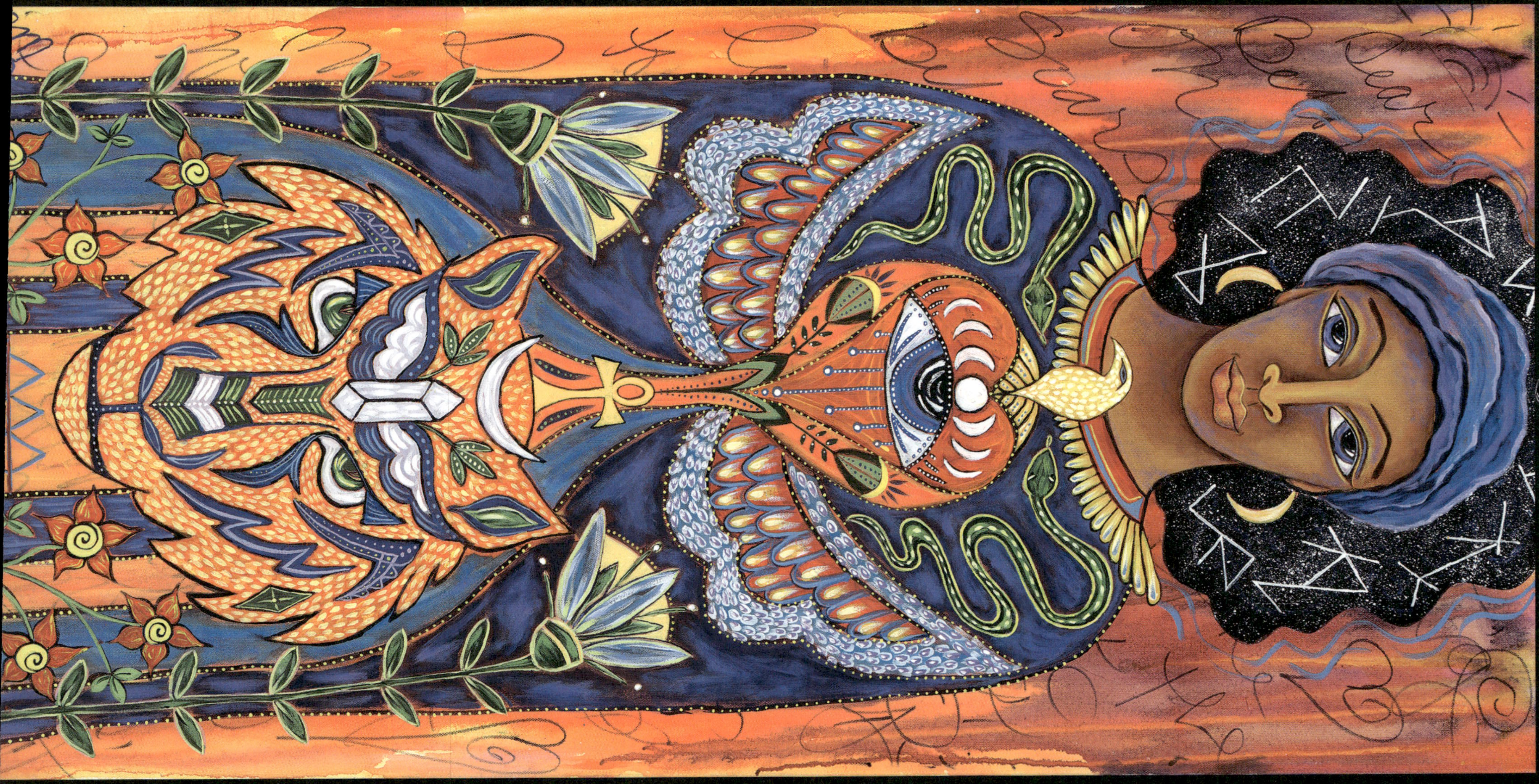

Reclaiming My Magic *© Suzanne Grace Michell 2023*

May

Make magic, stir the cauldron,
boil the brew, weave the tapestry,
wield the words, fire the forge.

I can feel the voice wanting to burst forth. I can feel the voices of all women wanting to burst forth . . . in a growing rumble of thunder . . . in a towering tidal wave breaking from the dam. The dam cannot hold. I feel as a drop of water in that wave with all my sisters.

Let us roll out on this titanic tide.
Women are writing a new story.

excerpt © Patricia Rose 2024

April 2027

S	M	T	W	T	F	S
				1	2	3
4	5	6	7	8	9	10
11	12	13	14	15	16	17
18	19	20	21	22	23	24
25	26	27	28	29	30	

June 2027

S	M	T	W	T	F	S
		1	2	3	4	5
6	7	8	9	10	11	12
13	14	15	16	17	18	19
20	21	22	23	24	25	26
27	28	29	30			

Sunday	Monday	Tuesday	Wednesday	Thursday	Friday	Saturday
						1 Beltane
2 ☽→♈	3	4	5 ☽→♉	6 ☉☌☽ New Moon in Taurus	7 ☽→♊	8 ☿→♊
9 ☽⚹♂ ☽→♋	10	11 ☽→♌	12 ☉□☽	13 ☽→♍	14 ♂→♍ ♀→♉	15 ☽→♎
16	17 ☽→♏	18	19	20 ☉☍☽ ☽→♐ ☉→♊ Full Moon in Scorpio Sun in Gemini	21	22 ☽→♑
23 / 30 ☽→♈	24 / 31	25 ☽→♒	26	27 ☽→♓	28 ☉□☽ ☿→♋	29

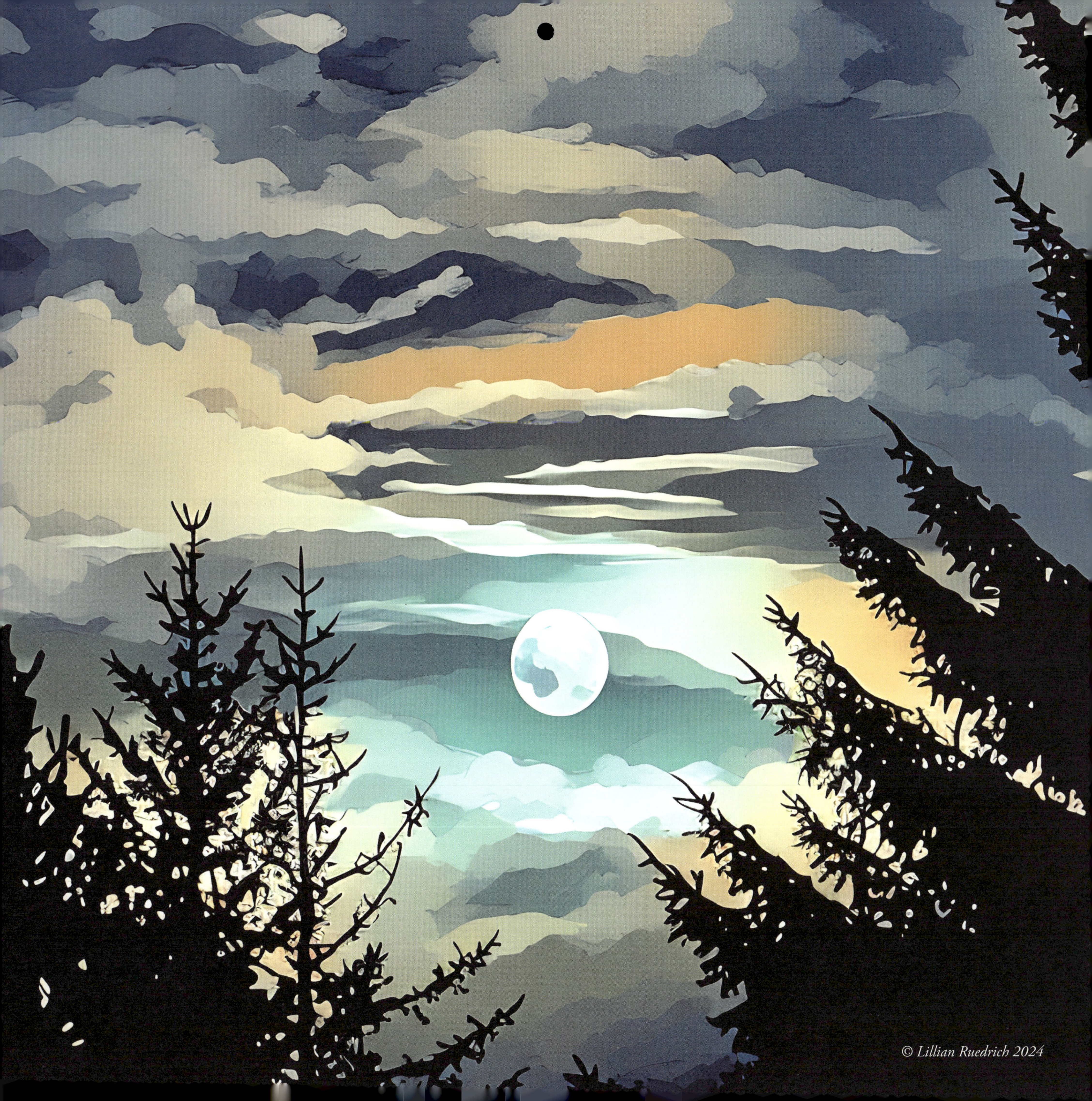

June

May 2027

S	M	T	W	T	F	S
						1
2	3	4	5	6	7	8
9	10	11	12	13	14	15
16	17	18	19	20	21	22
23	24	25	26	27	28	29
30	31					

July 2027

S	M	T	W	T	F	S
				1	2	3
4	5	6	7	8	9	10
11	12	13	14	15	16	17
18	19	20	21	22	23	24
25	26	27	28	29	30	31

Sunday	Monday	Tuesday	Wednesday	Thursday	Friday	Saturday
		1 ☽→♉	2	3 ☽→♊	4 ☉☌☽ New Moon in Gemini	5 ☽→♋
6	7 ☽→♌	8 ♀→♊	9 ☽→♍	10 ☿R	11 ☉□☽ ☽→♎	12
13	14 ☽→♏	15	16 ☽→♐	17	18 ☉☍☽ ☽→♑ Full Moon in Sagittarius	19
20	21 ☉→♋ ☽→♒ Summer Solstice Sun in Cancer	22	23	24 ☽→♓	25	26 ☿→♊ ☽→♈ ☉□☽
27	28 ☽→♉	29	30 ☽→♊			

When the darkness of the world
seeps into your soul and spreads like a virus
remember, the moon is always full
even when we can't see it.

When you need hope to keep going, look up to the sky,
bathe in her light—whether you see it or not
then, reflect it back out into the world.
The moon is always full.
Always, always full.

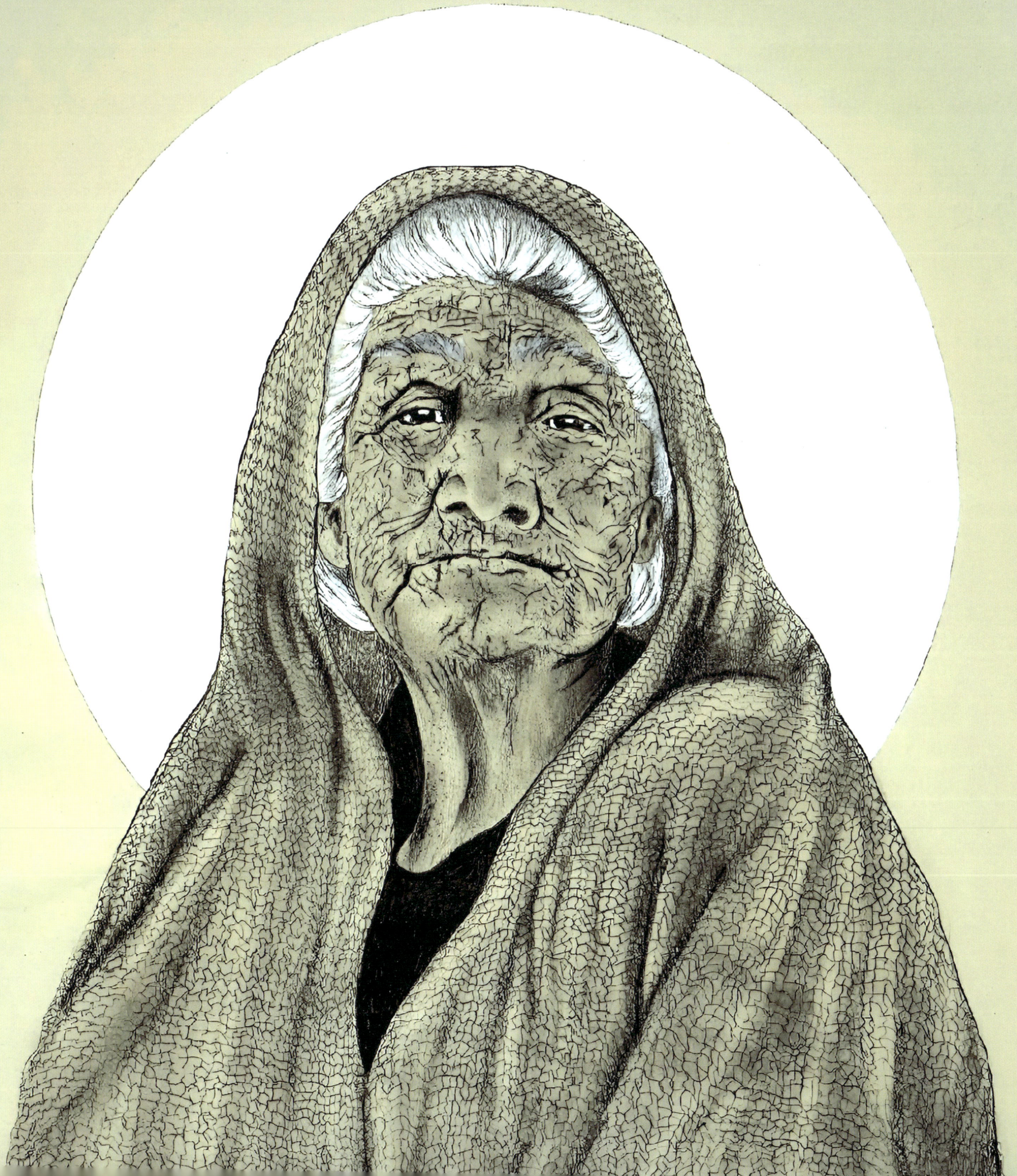

Dignidad / Dignity *© Carmen R Sonnes 2014*

July

A wise crone with 84 years of imagination
told me recently that
grief is love
with
no
place
to
go.
Pray the Love will outlast all the rest,
And sorrow will ebb with the tide
of our tomorrows.

excerpt © Colleen Joy Corbe' Percival 2025

June 2027

S	M	T	W	T	F	S
		1	2	3	4	5
6	7	8	9	10	11	12
13	14	15	16	17	18	19
20	21	22	23	24	25	26
27	28	29	30			

August 2027

S	M	T	W	T	F	S
1	2	3	4	5	6	7
8	9	10	11	12	13	14
15	16	17	18	19	20	21
22	23	24	25	26	27	28
29	30	31				

Sunday	Monday	Tuesday	Wednesday	Thursday	Friday	Saturday
				1	2 ♀→♋	3 ☽→♋ ☉☌☽ New Moon in Cancer
4 ☿D	5 ☽→♌	6	7 ☽→♍	8	9 ☽→♎ ♆R	10 ☉□☽
11 ☽→♏	12 ☿→♋	13 ☽→♐	14 ♂→♎	15	16 ☽→♑	17
18 ☉☍☽ ☽→♒ Full Moon in Capricorn	19	20	21 ☽→♓	22 ☉→♌ Sun in Leo	23 ☽→♈	24
25 ♃→♍	26 ☽→♉ ☉□☽	27 ♀→♌	28 ☽→♊	29	30 ☽→♋	31

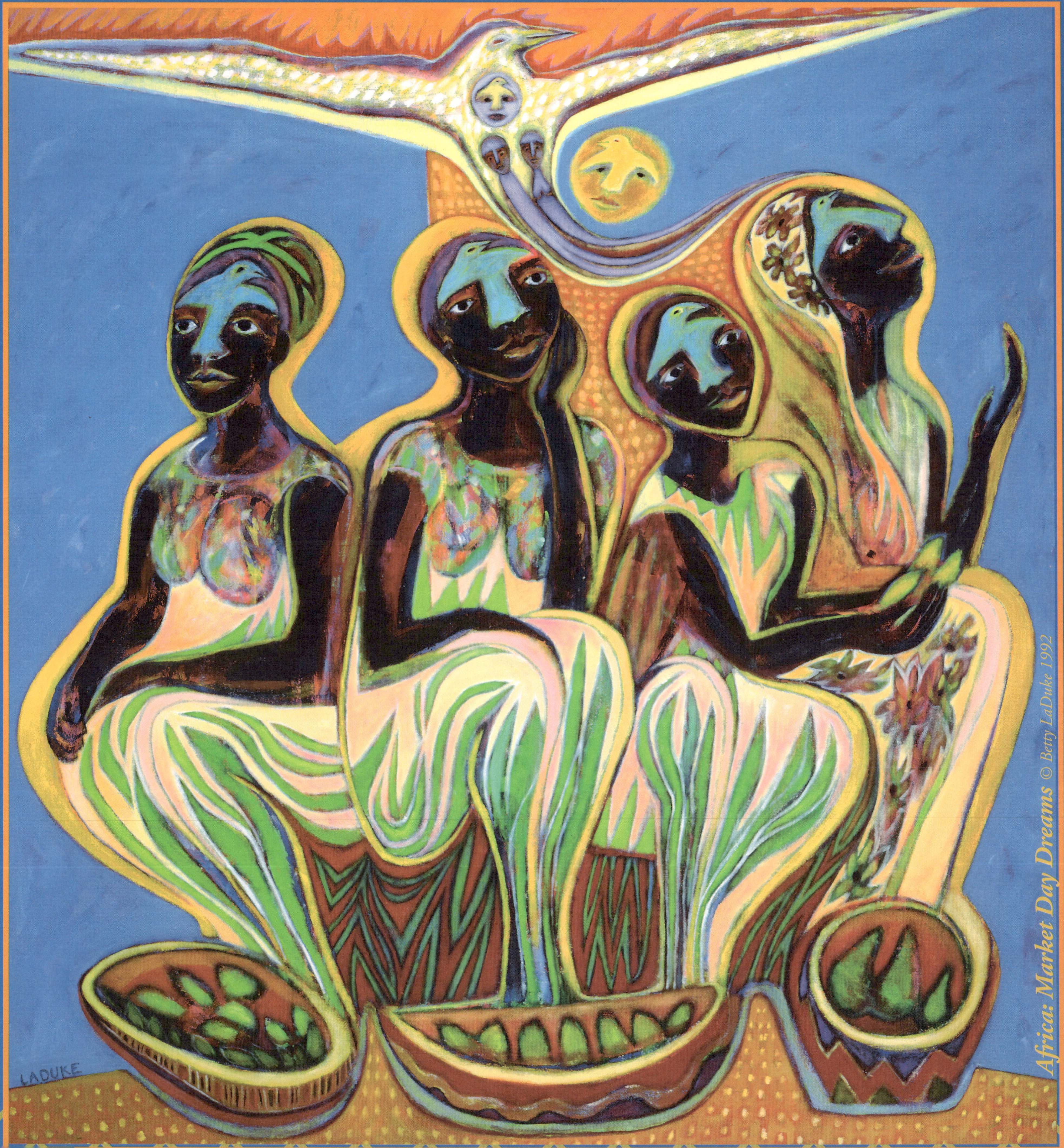

Africa: Market Day Dreams © Betty LaDuke 1992

August

Sunday	Monday	Tuesday	Wednesday	Thursday	Friday	Saturday
1 ☽→♌	2 ☉☌☽ ☿→♌ Lammas New Moon in Leo	3 ☽→♍	4	5 ☽→♎	6	7 ☽→♏ ⚷R
8 ☉□☽	9 ♄R ☽→♐	10	11	12 ☽→♑	13	14 ☽→♒
15	16 ☿→♍	17 ☉☍☽ ☽→♓ Lunar Lammas Full Moon in Aquarius	18	19 ☽→♈	20 ♀→♍	21
22 ☽→♉	23 ☉→♍ Sun in Virgo	24 ☽→♊ ☉□☽	25	26 ☽→♋	27	28 ☽→♌
29	30 ☽→♍	31 ☉☌☽ New Moon in Virgo Total Solar Eclipse				

July 2027

S	M	T	W	T	F	S
				1	2	3
4	5	6	7	8	9	10
11	12	13	14	15	16	17
18	19	20	21	22	23	24
25	26	27	28	29	30	31

September 2027

S	M	T	W	T	F	S
			1	2	3	4
5	6	7	8	9	10	11
12	13	14	15	16	17	18
19	20	21	22	23	24	25
26	27	28	29	30		

See the ancestor ways return.
See our own ways become a path
for a hopeful future.
We can be fierce. We can rage like a storm,
but we know when to be gentle.
how to speak quietly, steadily.
Most of all, we know what we want.
Gardens full of food and flowers.
Peace. Bounty. Sharing.

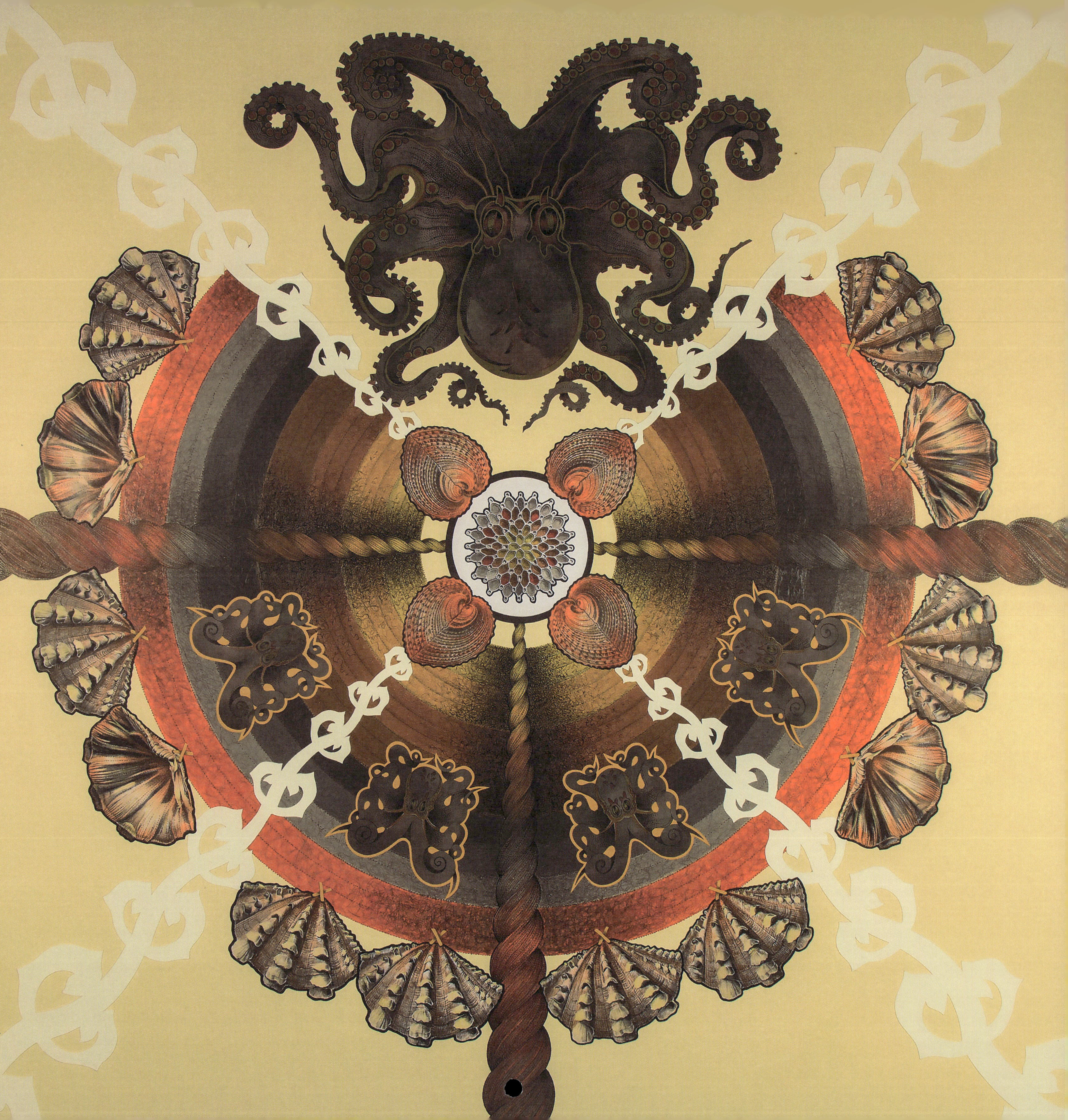

Tauranga Marae © Deborah K. Snider 2014

September

we shapeshift, find our new skins
revel under moonlit branches, let tethers fall away onto bedrock

we abandon everything to dark waters
save our shimmering essence, as the moon comes 'round

we wane together
lay our burning questions to cool in dwindling light

we'll find ourselves together once again, fully renewed
over & under the moon

excerpt ¤ Chris Cavan 2025

Sunday	Monday	Tuesday	Wednesday	Thursday	Friday	Saturday
			1 ♂→♏ ☽→♎	2	3 ☿→♎	4 ☽→♏
5	6 ☽→♐	7 ☉□☽	8 ☽→♑	9	10	11 ☽→♒
12	13 ♀→♎ ☽→♓	14	15 ♅R ☉☍☽ Full Moon in Pisces	16 ☽→♈	17	18 ☽→♉
19	20 ☽→♊	21	22 ☉→♎ Fall Equinox Sun in Libra	23 ☽→♋ ☉□☽	24	25 ☽→♌
26	27 ☿→♏ ☽→♍	28	29 ☽→♎ ☉☌☽ New Moon in Libra	30		

August 2027

S	M	T	W	T	F	S
1	2	3	4	5	6	7
8	9	10	11	12	13	14
15	16	17	18	19	20	21
22	23	24	25	26	27	28
29	30	31				

October 2027

S	M	T	W	T	F	S
					1	2
3	4	5	6	7	8	9
10	11	12	13	14	15	16
17	18	19	20	21	22	23
24	25	26	27	28	29	30
31						

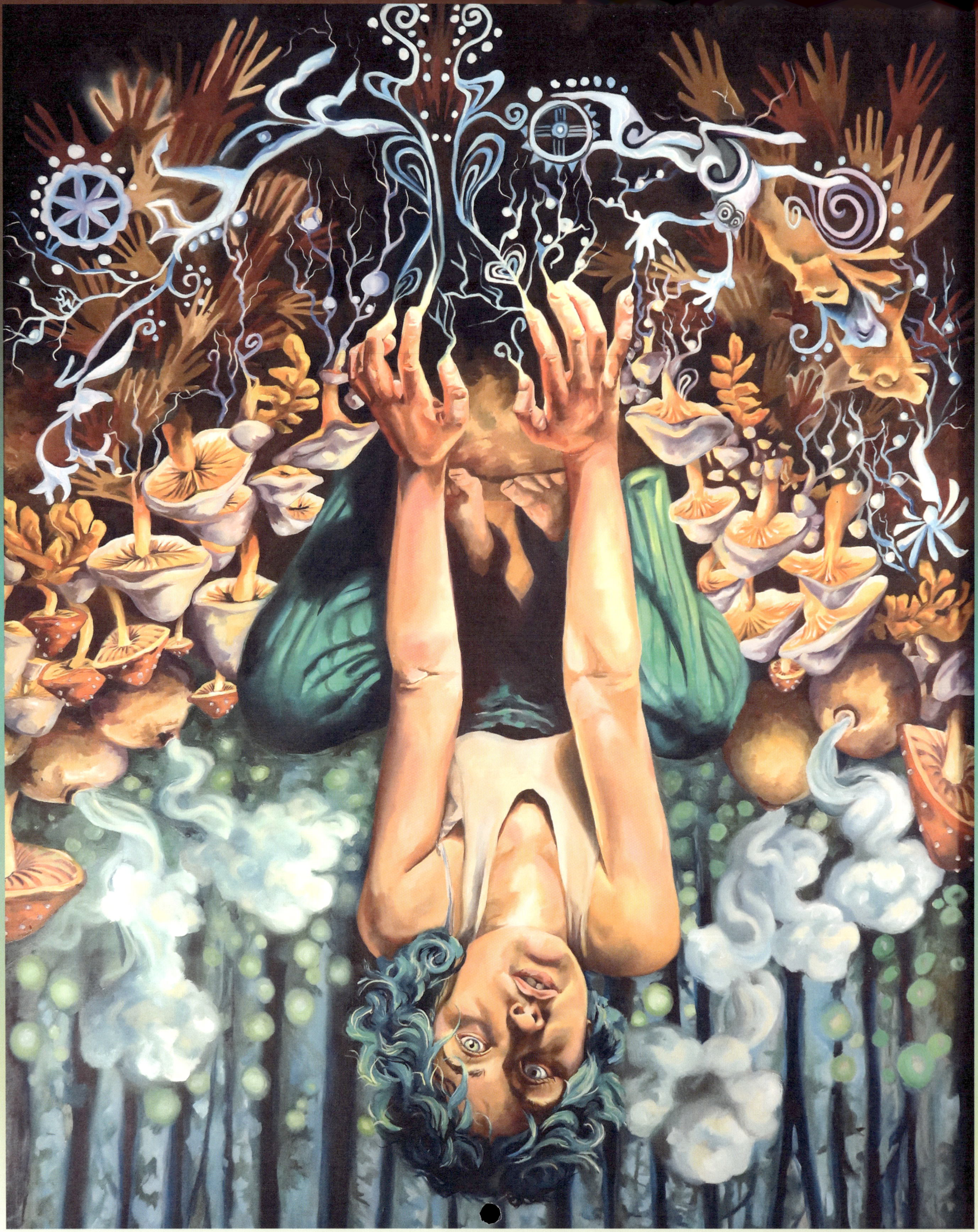

Ancestral Memory © Melissa Stratton Pandina 2025

October

I have been root and thorn, shadow and flame,
gentle rain and raging storm.

And still, I rise.
Still, I bloom.
Still, I become.

For I am the child of cycles,
the daughter of dusk and dawn.
I am never finished.
I am always new.

excerpt © Tiffany Giasson 2023

September 2027

S	M	T	W	T	F	S
			1	2	3	4
5	6	7	8	9	10	11
12	13	14	15	16	17	18
19	20	21	22	23	24	25
26	27	28	29	30		

November 2027

S	M	T	W	T	F	S
	1	2	3	4	5	6
7	8	9	10	11	12	13
14	15	16	17	18	19	20
21	22	23	24	25	26	27
28	29	30				

Sunday	Monday	Tuesday	Wednesday	Thursday	Friday	Saturday
					1 ☽→♏	2
3 ☽→♐	4	5	6 ☽→♑	7 ☉□☽ ☿R ♀→♏	8 ☽→♒	9
10	11 ☽→♓	12	13 ☽→♈	14	15 ☉☍☽ ♂→♐ ☽→♉ Full Moon in Aries	16 ☿→♎
17 ♇D	18 ☽→♊	19	20 ☽→♋	21	22 ☉□☽ ☽→♌	23 ☉→♏ Sun in Scorpio
24 ☽→♍ ☽→♐ 31 Samhain / Hallowmas	25	26 ☽→♎	27	28 ☿D ☽→♏	29 ☉☌☽ Lunar Samhain New Moon in Scorpio	30

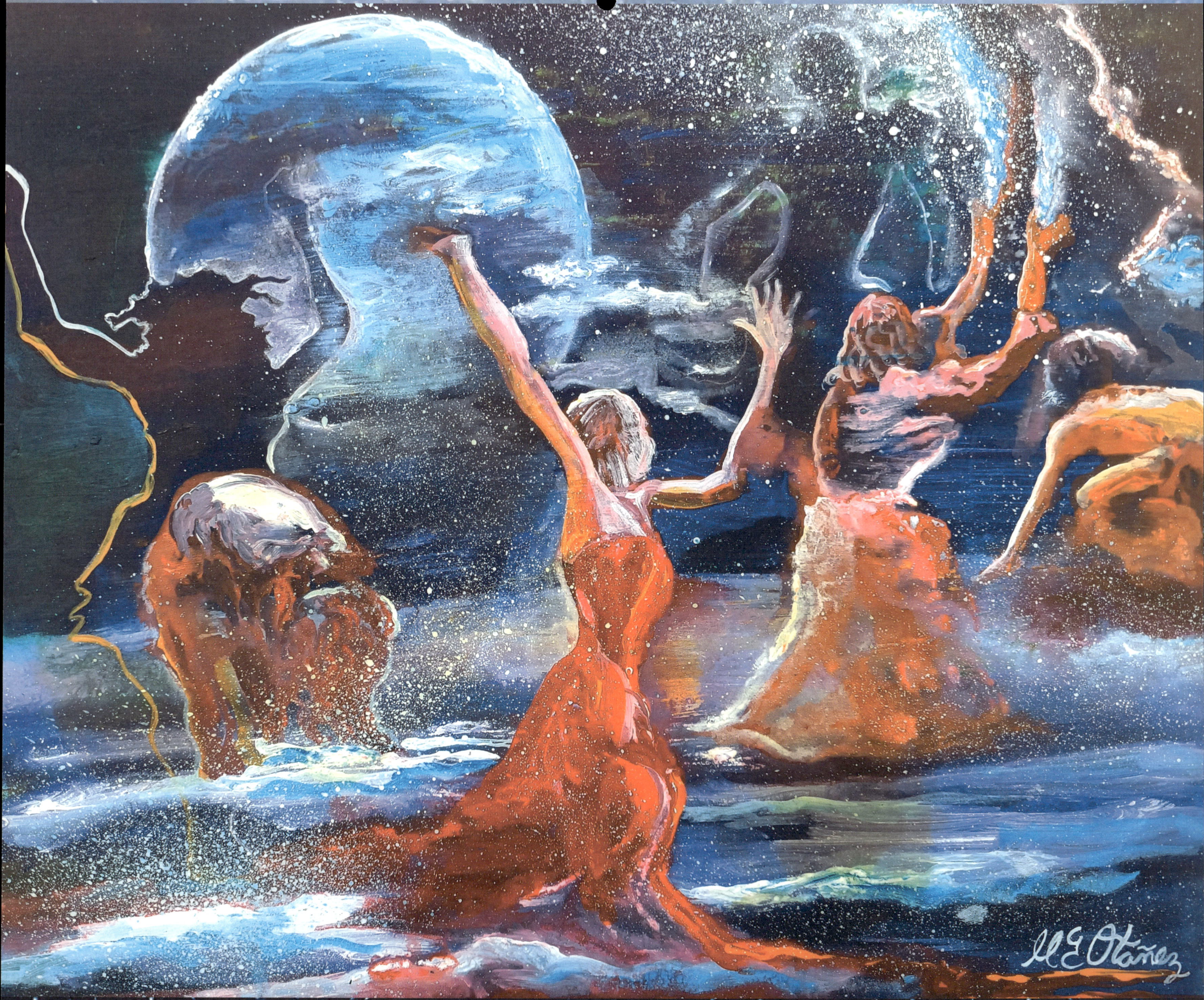

La Danza de Renovación *© Niurka Guzmán Otañez 2022*

November

Sunday	Monday	Tuesday	Wednesday	Thursday	Friday	Saturday
	1 ♀→♐	2 ☽→♑	3	4 ☽→♒	5	6 ☉□☽
7 ☽→♓ Daylight Saving Time Ends 2:00 am	8	9 ☿→♏ ☽→♈	10	11	12 ☽→♉	13 ☉☍☽ Full Moon in Taurus
14 ☽→♊	15	16 ☽→♋	17	18 ☽→♌	19	20 ☉□☽ ☽→♍
21	22 ☉→♐ ☽→♎ Sun in Sagittarius	23	24	25 ☽→♏ ♀→♑ ♂→♑	26	27 ☽→♐ ☉☌☽ New Moon in Sagittarius
28	29 ☿→♐ ☽→♑	30				

October 2027

S	M	T	W	T	F	S
					1	2
3	4	5	6	7	8	9
10	11	12	13	14	15	16
17	18	19	20	21	22	23
24	25	26	27	28	29	30
31						

December 2027

S	M	T	W	T	F	S
			1	2	3	4
5	6	7	8	9	10	11
12	13	14	15	16	17	18
19	20	21	22	23	24	25
26	27	28	29	30	31	

I have heard that when we die
we kiss the moon and dance the sky
so grab your drum and circle round
and help me draw the heavens down

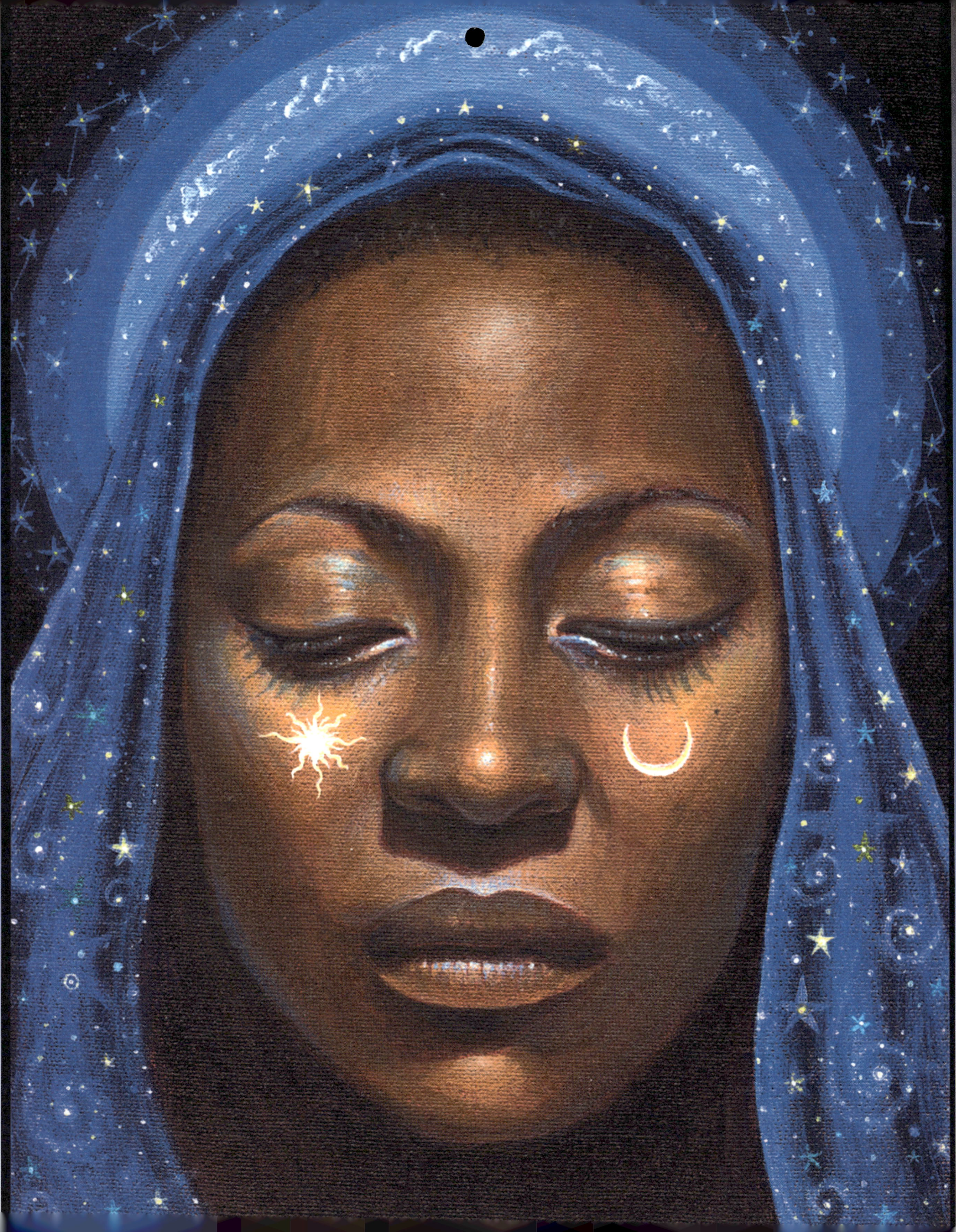

Queen of Heaven © Emily Kell 2025

December

whatever you are struggling with
lay it down for me here daughter
rest your heavy bones
upon my ancient shores
let the light of the moon
penetrate the depths of your pain
cleanse and clear
whatever ails you my daughter
lay it down for me here
all of you is welcome
¤ *Tasha Zigerelli 2017*

November 2027

S	M	T	W	T	F	S
	1	2	3	4	5	6
7	8	9	10	11	12	13
14	15	16	17	18	19	20
21	22	23	24	25	26	27
28	29	30				

Sunday	Monday	Tuesday	Wednesday	Thursday	Friday	Saturday
			1	2 ☽→♒	3	4 ☽→♓
5 ☉□☽	6	7 ☽→♈	8	9 ☽→♉	10	11 ☽→♊
12	13 ☉☍☽ ☽→♋ Full Moon in Gemini	14	15 ♆D ☽→♌	16	17	18 ☽→♍ ☿→♑
19 ♀→♒	20 ☉□☽ ☽→♎	21 ☉→♑ Winter Solstice Sun in Capricorn	22 ☽→♏	23 ♄D	24 ☽→♐	25
26	27 ☽→♑ ☉☌☽ New Moon in Capricorn	28	29 ☽→♒	30	31	

January 2028

S	M	T	W	T	F	S
						1
2	3	4	5	6	7	8
9	10	11	12	13	14	15
16	17	18	19	20	21	22
23	24	25	26	27	28	29
29	31					

Moon Transits

The Moon changes signs every 2½ days. The sign that the Moon is in sets the emotional tone of the day.

♒ Moon in Aquarius calls us to the circle and away from private concerns; it reminds us of the sacredness of collaboration and collectivity. It's time to search for new allies, to network, and to live our philosophy.

♓ Moon in Pisces makes us aware, sometimes painfully, of our emotions. It heightens compassion, intuition. We may have to strengthen boundaries. Explore the temple of imagination.

♈ Moon in Aries accesses our fire; temper, impatience and passion. We feel an urgency to focus, but we can lose our empathy. It's time to do what truly makes us feel alive, to initiate projects and set boundaries.

♉ Moon in Taurus slows us down; roots grow deep in this stubborn, creative, sensual time. It's time to cultivate our earthly resources: garden, home, and body. Plant seeds in fertile loam, listen to the Earth's magic.

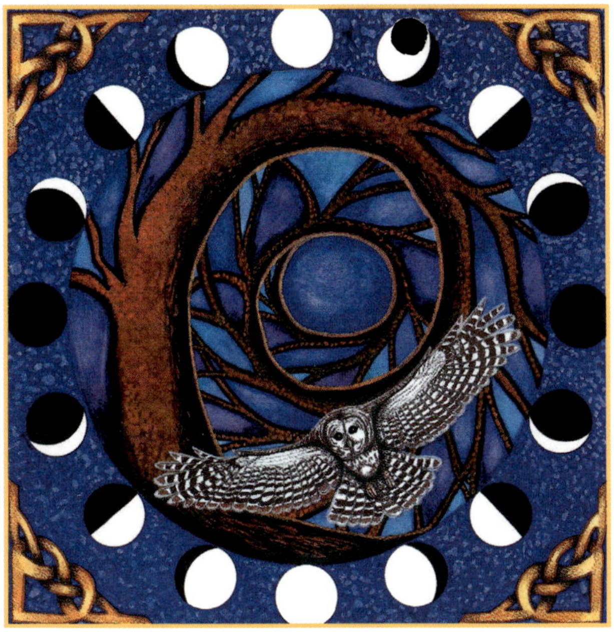

The Passage *© Megan Welti 2018*

♊ Moon in Gemini speeds our thoughts and nerves. It's time to weave words: talk, listen, laugh, sing and write. Network, negotiate, rearrange; juggle possibilities; just don't get spread too thin.

♋ Moon in Cancer reconnects us with our emotions. We may get overwhelmed and defensive, or we can nourish ourselves and reconnect with our true feelings. Water is healing; bathe, hydrate, make soup.

♌ Moon in Leo gets us into the heart of the action. It's time to let our light shine, express ourselves and appreciate other's unique stories. Celebrate, ritualize, dramatize. Share with true Leonine generosity.

♍ Moon in Virgo sharpens our minds and nerves. It helps us digest information and assess the situation. Invoke Virgoan compassion and brilliant problem-solving. Clean, organize, edit, weed and heal.

♎ Moon in Libra warms our hearts and heightens our aesthetics. Beauty, fairness and balance feed us. We want everyone to get along, and we become allergic to discord in the culture and with our beloveds.

♏ Moon in Scorpio turns us inward, deepens our curiosity and focus, but gives us attitude. We need privacy, as moods may be prickly. Clear the deadwood of soul or garden. Seek deep, refreshing contemplation.

♐ Moon in Sagittarius gets us moving around the globe, or into our minds. It loans us fresh (often tactless) honesty, an adventurous spark, philosophical perspective and easy rapport with the natural world.

♑ Moon in Capricorn whets our ambition and tests our sense of humor. It's time to put sweat-equity into our dreams; organize, build, manifest. Set clear short-term goals and feel the joy of accomplishment.

adapted from Heather Roan Robbins' Moon Signs and Moon Transits *© Mother Tongue Ink 2020*

Constellations of the Zodiac

These stations of the zodiac were named thousands of years ago for the constellations that were behind them at the time. The signs of the zodiac act like a light filter, coloring the qualities of life force. As the Sun, Moon and other planets move through the zodiac, the following influences are energized:

♒ Aquarius (Air): Community, ingenuity, collaboration, idealism. It's time to honor the philosophy of love and the power of community.

♓ Pisces (Water): Introspection, imagination, sensitivity and intuition. We process and gestate our dreams.

♈ Aries (Fire): Brave, direct, rebellious, energized. Our inner teenager comes alive; our adult self needs to direct the energy wisely.

♉ Taurus (Earth): Sensual, rooted, nurturing, material manifestation. We slow down, get earthy, awaken our senses, begin to build, form roots, and stubborn strength.

♊ Gemini (Air): Communication, networking, curiosity, quick witted. We connect with like minds and build a network of understanding.

♋ Cancer (Water): Family, home, emotional awareness, nourishment. We need time in our shell and with our familiars.

♌ Leo (Fire): Creativity, charisma, warmth, and enthusiasm. Gather with others to celebrate and share bounty.

♍ Virgo (Earth): Mercurial, curious, critical, and engaged. The mood sharpens our minds and nerves, and sends us back to work.

♎ Libra (Air): Beauty, equality, egalitarianism, cooperation. We grow more friendly, relationship oriented, and incensed by injustice.

♏ Scorpio (Water): Sharp focus, perceptive, empowered, mysterious. The mood is smoky, primal, occult, and curious; still waters run deep.

♐ Sagittarius (Fire): Curiosity, honesty, exploration, playfulness. We grow more curious about what's unfamiliar.

♑ Capricorn (Earth): family, history, dreams, traditions. We need mountains to climb and problems to solve.

adapted from Heather Roan Robbins' Sun Signs and Sun Transits *© Mother Tongue Ink 2016*

Herbs for Over the Moon

Rest, brave one. Pause and trust the stability of your internal foundation. Choose to be in this moment, fully. Pulsatilla*, we lift you to the waning Gibbous moon and together we take 3 drops: one drop for the unwavering Mother, one drop for the ethers and one drop for those of us that live in between the two. Compassionately navigate us through the trenches and soften all our doubts, fears and worries.

Ease into gentle surrender. Invite in the tonifying, yin energy of shatavari and ashwagandha. Let their presence calm, soothe and nourish you. Transmit to your nervous system that you are safe. Acknowledge your lymphatic system for protecting your bodies and for being an emotional filter. Commit to tending to its subtle waters as we make our descent into the constricted and restricted parts of ourselves.

Wise plant spirits, we call you in one by one during this time of deactivation and truthful exploration. Milky oats, nourish us and help repair the frayed parts. Ocotillo bark, clear all physical and emotional congestion. Orange peel, help us digest what is about to surface. Hawthorne berry, tune our heart spaces to the frequency of self compassion and love. Motherwort, we ask that you increase the calm and help us stand fully in our courage as we take inventory.

In the safety of this container, at your own perfect pace, explore the following:

- What truths are you being with in this moment? What is lurking in the shadows?
- Do you have forms of emotional release that feel restorative?
- Do you have time and space in your life that feels sacred?
- Do you have as many deep, meaningful interactions with others as you like?
- What do you desire to be intact so you can be the boldest, most vital version of yourself?

Center your responses and desires. Let your programming begin to unravel. Release toxic connections by making clean cuts. Design the way forward from your biggest imagination. Decide now and if it scares you, do it afraid. Prioritize your flourishing and center your livingness.

Karen L. Culpepper © Mother Tongue Ink 2026

**Pulsatilla is a drop dose herb. My request is that you explore it (and all plants) with respect and care. Lean into guidance through research, being with the spirit of the plant and/or with a practitioner who has experience with the essence and impact of the plant's potency.*

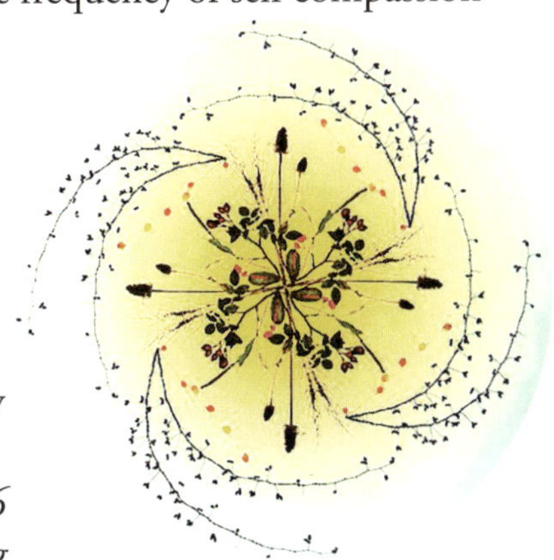

© Maria Silmon 2014

Lunar Year of the Fire Sheep: 2027

Chinese New Year begins on the second new Moon after Winter Solstice. The new Moon on February 6 begins the year of the Sheep. The Year of the Sheep can be a time of peace, calm, and contentment. Family, close friends, and intimacy are valued. The hectic pace of life can slow down, and people are more caring, sensitive, and emotional. The arts will flourish and creativity will flow, but refined beauty and elegance is expensive and debt may easily accrue. "Sheep eat paper," meaning that Sheep can overspend money.

Wemoon born in Sheep years (1919, 1931, 1943, 1955, 1967, 1979, 1991, 2003, 2015, 2027) are peaceful, creative, and compassionate souls. They have strong intuition, excel in creative fields, and are known for their gentle, kind-hearted, and artistic nature. They are often thoughtful, empathetic, and possess a strong inner resilience, preferring a quiet life of harmony. Over time, a Sheep wemoon's kindness can achieve powerful results, making old age the best time of a Sheep wemoon's life, when she is a crone.

Of the five Taoist elements Fire, Earth, Metal, Water, and Wood, 2027 is a Fire year. Fire adds boldness and passion to the receptive Sheep making this an excellent year to express your creativity and explore the arts. Your artistic endeavors and humanitarian efforts will be successful. This is a favorable year for teamwork, collaborative environments, and social understanding, although the element Fire can also bring periods of impulsiveness or emotional intensity.

Sheep is also translated as Goat or Ram. But Ram is a Yang symbol of masculinity, and Sheep is essentially Yin. Ram could be confused with the Western sign of Aries the Ram, and Sheep has little of Aries' innate fiery energy. Instead, Aries correlates to the mighty Dragon. Goat may evoke the Western sign of Capricorn the Goat, but Sheep rarely possess the drive or ambition to ascend to the mountaintop like Capricorn which corresponds to steady Ox. Sheep correlates to the Western sign Cancer, the sign of the mother and nurturer. Sheep is most compatible with another Sheep, Rabbit, Horse, and Pig.

Susan Levitt © Mother Tongue Ink 2026

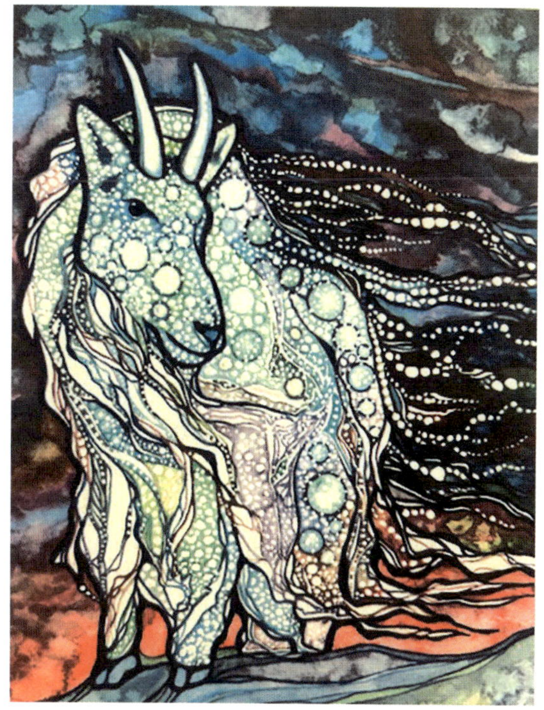

Mountain Spirit *© Tamara Phillips 2015*

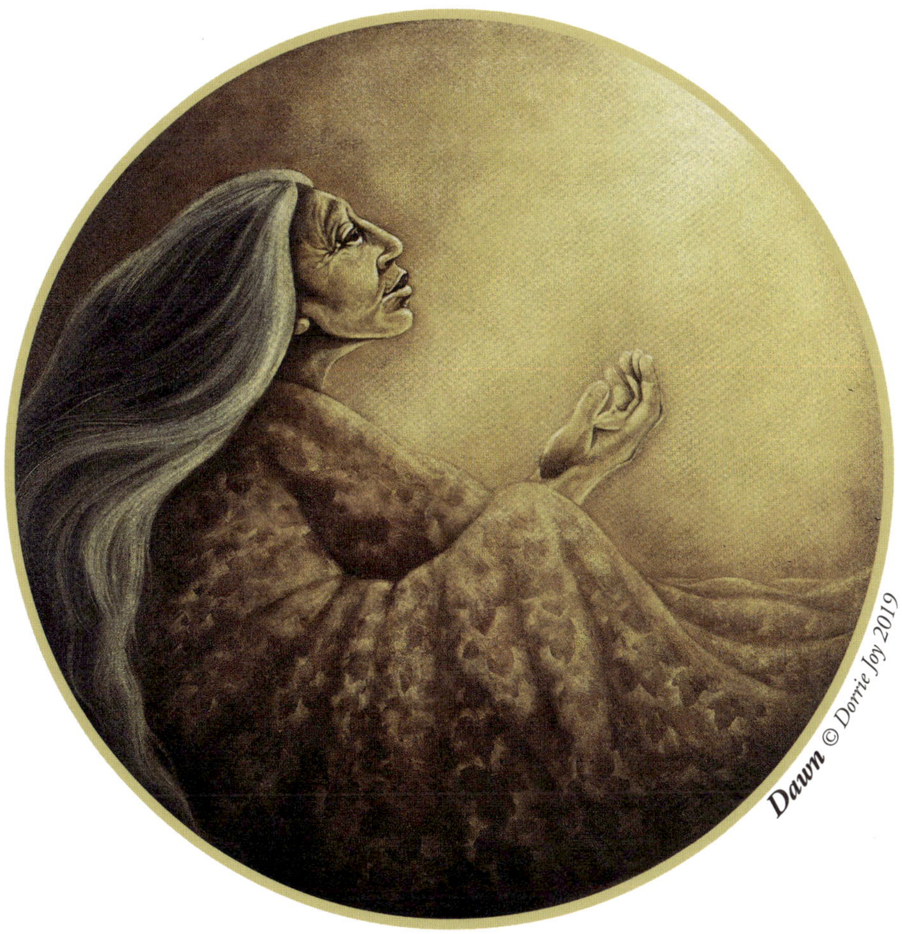

Dawn *© Dorrie Joy 2019*

Eclipses: 2027

Solar and Lunar Eclipses occur when the Earth, Sun and Moon align at the Moon's nodal axis, usually four times a year, during New and Full Moons, respectively. The South (past) and North (future) Nodes symbolize our evolutionary path. Eclipses catalyze destiny's calling. Use eclipse degrees in your birth chart to identify potential release points.

February 6: The Aånnular Solar Eclipse at 18° Aquarius offers us the opportunity for reflection on our community care projects. Feed involvements with your own unique inspirations. Gather the good.

February 20: The Penumbral Lunar Eclipse at 2° Virgo brings focus on the health of body, mind and spirit. Renew commitments to practices that balance and strengthen your system.

July 18: The Penumbral Lunar Eclipse at 26° Capricorn taps into our need to matter. Let the emerging light cast off shadows. Embrace youår authenticity.

August 2: When the Total Solar Eclipse at 14° Leo illuminates the shadows, look deeply within to find insights about that which has alluded you. Then light up with fresh awareness of your true colors.

August 17: On the Penumbral Lunar Eclipse at 24°, let Aquarius speak truth to your inner power, then allow renewed light to bring right relationship with outer power.

Mercury Retrogrades: 2027

Mercury, planetary muse and mentor of our mental and communicative lives, appears to reverse its course three or four times a year. We may experience less stress during these periods by taking the time to pause and go back over familiar territory, giving second thoughts to dropped projects or miscommunications. Get proactive with mechanical safety and maintenance. It's time to "recall the now" of the past and deal with underlying issues. Leave matters that lock in future commitments until Mercury goes direct.

Mercury has three retrograde periods this year, beginning in Water signs and ending in Air signs.

February 9–March 3: When Mercury retreats in Pisces, let tensions release, and give yourself some extra space. Go by feel, especially at the Full Moon on February 20, and allow yourself to be seen anew.

June 10–July 4: As Mercury goes back over familiar territory in Cancer, find dropped stitches, lost words and unkept promises. Then make a new way, truer and wiser. The Full Moon on June 18 offers clues.

October 7–28: It's time to shift conditions within yourself when Mercury retraces its path in Scorpio. Reorganize what is out of place. Practice not saying everything you think. Level up in maturity with the Full Moon on October 15.

Sandra Pastorius © Mother Tongue Ink 2026

Tarot for 2027:
Over the Moon and Beyond

Tarot wisdom for 2027 tells us how brave we can be when armed with passion for truth and justice. We will have opportunities to be Lioness, Mother-Leader, Priestess . . . even the Moon Woman who welcomes change. These coming days provide endless moments inspiring strength, commitment and the heart to go beyond anything we have thought, done or dreamed about before.

We determine the Tarot of the year by adding its numbers. Thus 2027 gives us 11, *Courage*, and in some decks, *Justice*. With the first ten cards —over the past ten years—the Tarot has led us on a journey to discover our Path and Purpose. We began as the innocent *Fool* and traveled, experiencing many Earthly aspects, to and through the *Wheel of Fortune*.

Now things have shifted. This year we dare to move to the edge. During 2027, we leave our safe places behind and, armed with the intuitive and creative Mysteries of the moon, step out into our solar system and even into other realms and dimensions. Choose a favorite constellation to learn about and meditate on this year, the one you search for on clear midnights: the Pleiades, Cassiopeia, Ursa Major, Cygnus the Swan. The Universe beckons and offers wisdom that we might bring home to change our world.

Even the physical picture of the number Eleven is instructive. It creates twin pillars, a space to walk, dance, run, or tiptoe through. A great meditation for 2027 is to sit quietly focusing on breath. Then count to ten and envision what the twin pillars might look like. They might be Grecian columns. They might be stone-upon-stone. They could be wooden, roughhewn or detailed like a Totem Pole. They could be neon. Bare, painted brightly or twined with vines.

With our next breath, we move through them to a place nearby or in another universe. It might be a path diaphanous as the Milky Way. It could look like a village of celestial homes made of prisms. Or it could be a street with our childhood home, a seashore vacation, a forest we visited in dreams. We might encounter a Spirit Guide, angel, or dear one who has crossed over. They may whisper a message to us.

When we repeat this practice, our envisioning changes, as does what we hear and receive. The ultimate goal is to perceive a direction both for ourselves and for our Earth this year. Keep a journal of your Pillar Visions. Use them to create poems, stories, sketches, or the lyrics of a song.

Since the elements of eleven are abstract, I have seen this card illustrated in a myriad of ways. Often with a lion, the symbol of courage. Or with a figure known for bravery like Joan of Arc. Who is the bravest person you have ever known? Or read about? Choose a figure whose character you would like to emulate during 2027. Or pick an animal who protects her tribe and its vulnerable ones. Make this creature your totem.

When reading Tarot, I am inspired by the minor arcana along with the archetypes of the major cards. The meaning of the suit cards contains echoes of their major equivalents. Eleven, then, just beyond ten, is represented by Pages. These young people exemplify innocence and curiosity, dedication to service, the desire to learn. How do they take us over the moon?

The *Page of Swords* entices us to master something logical and practical, maybe another language, or a useful skill. The *Page of Wands* encourages us to pursue a psychic or artistic gift, one we are interested in even if we feel we don't have "talent." Our true talents come with dedication and daring. Once we step into the shadow, magically, everything becomes clear!

The *Youth of Pentacles* calls us to the physical world, our beautiful planet! What can we do this year to honor all the living things around us? How can we learn to notice more, relate better, truly engage with the environment? And finally the *Squire of Cups*. Young adult emotions are so raw and changeable, just like the moon! This year never be afraid to feel pain and joy, sorrow and ecstasy.

Tarot for 2027 would not be complete without a further look at the numbers. All double digits resolve into a single one. Thus eleven becomes two, which, in the Major Arcana, is the *High Priestess*. I also find it fascinating that the numbers for Major Archetypal cards are often written in Roman numerals. Thus 2 becomes II, visually so close to eleven. Tarot is endlessly magical, full of double-entendre and even humor!

For me the figure of the *High Priestess* is the ultimate guardian of the Crown Chakra, Guide into other dimensions, realities, life beyond this Earthly One. Her symbol is the moon with all its shadowy doorways. She empowers us to find and embrace our psychic abilities.

What does it really mean to be psychic? This is a deeply individual question. I have learned from years of reading palms, that each of us connects with Spirit differently. This often aligns with the "clairs." Some are clairvoyant, visionary. Others receive words and phrases or music, clairaudient. There are those of us who "just know" through clairsentience, the sensitive antenna within our bodies. And there are others whose strong connection to the heart lifts them through pure Love.

The one, single, universal characteristic of really stepping into psychic mode is to totally get rid of self and become an open channel to and from Spirit. We allow Life Force Energy to flow through us to enliven our precious world.

It can be terrifying to let go completely—and we can't live continuously in this state. But through meditation, breath, noticing the essential nature of this world, of the cycles and renewal, of Love for another and for self, the year 2027 offers such moments. If . . .

If we dare to step off the cliff of everything safe, what we know, what is literal. The old teachings contain wisdoms—the oldest ones most. But this is the year we understand truth at the edges, rim of the moon. We balance there. If we fall, we fall. If we fall with an open, trusting heart, we fly.

Joanne M. Clarkson © Mother Tongue Ink 2026

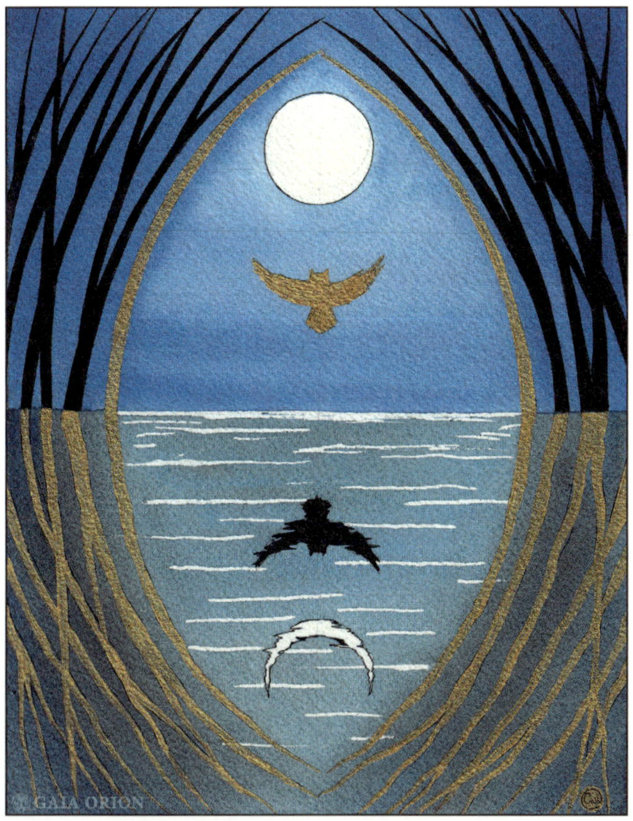

Beyond the Veil © Gaia Orion 2024

Astrological Year at a Glance Introduction

In *All About Love*, bell hooks wrote that "rarely, if ever, are any of us healed in isolation." She wasn't only speaking about romantic love, but about the radical act of creating spaces where care circulates—where the self expands through community rather than shrinking for survival. Audre Lorde, too, reminds us that "without community, there is no liberation," that our power is neither born nor sustained in antisocialism.

2027 carries that lesson like a heartbeat—constant and consistent.

On January 10, Mars turns retrograde in Virgo, prompting an honest reckoning with how we spend our energy. Have our offerings become performance, or prayer? True devotion to our craft, our cause, or our healing requires rhythm, not hustle. With Saturn, Neptune, and Chiron all in Aries, the collective begins the year reexamining what selfhood really means. Independence is no longer the prize—integrity is.

When Chiron enters Taurus on April 14, the body becomes our next teacher. Healing turns sensual and somatic: the softness of soil, the warmth of shared meals, the courage to rest without guilt. *Healing happens in communion*—hooks' reminder echoes—*through hands that tend and voices that soothe*.

Meanwhile, Pluto retrogrades in Aquarius in May, asking us to reflect on how our collective progress truly serves the whole. Revolution without empathy becomes psychological mimicry. As Neptune turns retrograde in Aries on July 9, we begin to see through illusions of hyper-independence. Around July 25, Jupiter's shift from Leo to Virgo reorients wisdom toward service: to create not for applause, but for alignment.

Later in the year, Uranus retrograde in Gemini on September 15 keeps revolution alive through dialogue. How we speak, organize, and share information will determine how the future breathes. Lorde once wrote that "the master's tools will never dismantle the master's house," and this year invites us to build new tools altogether—ones forged from empathy, collaboration, and critical joy.

By December 15, Neptune turns direct, and on December 23, Saturn follows. The cosmic tone softens into renewal. Healing and liberation reveal themselves not as distant ideals but as daily practices—conversations, choices, and collective care rituals. The astrology of 2027 doesn't just ask us to become ourselves; it asks us to become ourselves *together*.

Monisha Holmes © Mother Tongue Ink 2026

Life is a balancing act! Fortunately, we can look for guidance to the Signs of the Zodiac, a coherent symbolic system for wholistic living. The twelve Signs illuminate a path of self-actualization for the seeker, and are composed of six pairs of opposite and counter-balancing Signs, (the opposition aspect is 180° apart).

Each of these six axes represents the interplay of life principles in our quest for living the full cycle of life in an integrated, meaningful way. We become skillful "jugglers of paradox" as we face the inevitable dilemmas and contradictions in our experience and learn to allow other points of view to balance our perspectives and initiate fresh approaches, finding the middle way. It is through our struggles to reconcile these polarities that we develop a healthy psyche, and a coherency for authentic expression. Mirroring the brain's emphasis on hemispheric synthesis, we learn integration through expressing attributes of both sides in a dynamic reciprocity, engaging both our uniqueness and our universality.

As you explore the various positions you may hold on each axis, allow reciprocating dialogs to expand your awareness. We can balance various Sign excesses or deficiencies through using metaphorical corrective measures. Muse on the reminders below to guide and enchant your journey with a sense of perspective and purpose.

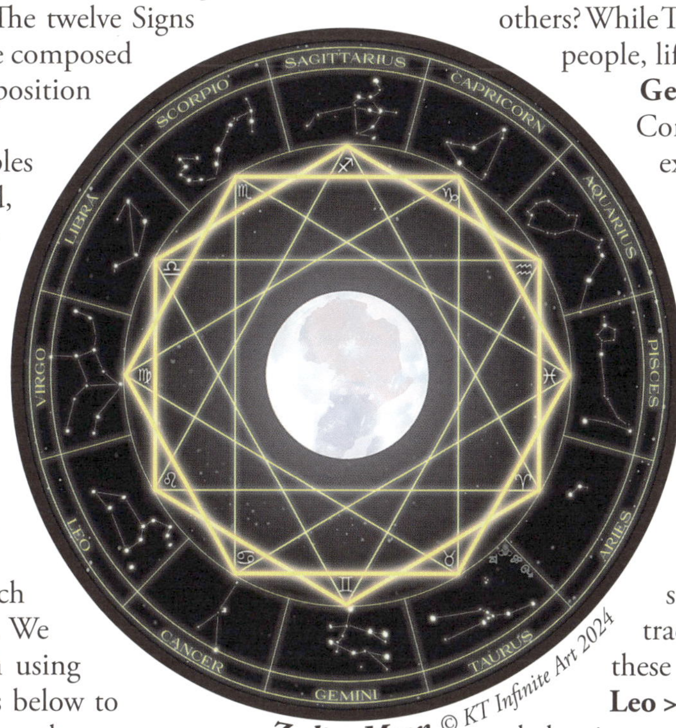

Zodiac Moon *© KT Infinite Art 2024*

Aries > 1 < Libra—Engage in dialogs about Relatedness. We come into life through Aries, boldly open and full of fire energy, fresh with *chi*. We are dependent upon the gaze from "another" throughout our life, to witness, as shadow or as beloved. Very early we puzzle, *how am I changed by my positions as self / other and subject / object?* Libra symbolizes this mirroring and projecting dynamic throughout life. Play "hide and seek". Enjoy being found.

Taurus > 2 < Scorpio—Engage in dialogs about Embodiment. Our hunger for growth and regeneration defines us on this axis of embodiment. How do we meet our needs for sustenance both physically and emotionally? What feeds us? How do we feed others? While Taurus retains, Scorpio relinquishes—food, possessions, values, people, life itself.

Gemini > 3 < Sagittarius—Engage in dialogs about Communications. Our curiosity fuels mental and physical explorations, and stimulates the interplay of learning from, and teaching one another. Gemini loves sharing intellectual connections among friends and peers, and enjoys a close association to the environment. Sagittarius takes the wide view, allowing opinions and categories to factor into allegiances and philosophies of belief. How can we simultaneously think globally and act locally?

Cancer > 4 < Capricorn—Engage in dialogs about Security. Along this axis we develop in kinship groups, growing a sense of belonging in our Cancerian private home and family space, and in the Capricornian hallways of our public work or service life. What is our commitment to standing strong on the foundations of our forbearers and the traditions they built? Who decides who belongs? The answers to these questions mean everything to the next generation.

Leo > 5 < Aquarius—Engage in dialogs about Creativity. Here the balancing act is between expressing a potency of Heart as our unique self, Leo, with a potency of Mind as a member of unique groups, Aquarius. Does our creativity serve both our sense of personal value and the collective common good? In what ways do we share consciousness?

Virgo > 6 < Pisces—Engage in dialogs about Healing. Conscious and unconscious motivations can transfix us, and at times hold sway over our freedom of expression. How can Virgo's devotion to order and duty help keep our practical affairs in control, while attending with trust and compassion to Pisces' soulful longings? Hold the other in highest esteem.

Sandra Pastorius © Mother Tongue Ink 2026

SIGNS AND SYMBOLS AT A GLANCE

♈ **Aries**
♉ **Taurus**
♊ **Gemini**
♋ **Cancer**
♌ **Leo**
♍ **Virgo**
♎ **Libra**
♏ **Scorpio**
♐ **Sagittarius**
♑ **Capricorn**
♒ **Aquarius**
♓ **Pisces**

PERSONAL PLANETS

are closest to Earth.

☉ **Sun:** self radiating outward, character, ego
☽ **Moon:** inward sense of self, emotions, psyche
☿ **Mercury:** communication, travel, thought
♀ **Venus:** relationship, love, sense of beauty, empathy
♂ **Mars:** will to act, initiative, ambition

SOCIAL PLANETS

are between personal and outer planets.

♃ **Jupiter:** expansion, opportunities, leadership
♄ **Saturn:** limits, structure, discipline
Note: the seven days of the week are named after the above seven heavenly bodies.
⚷ **Chiron:** a small planetary body between Saturn and Uranus representing the wounded healer

TRANSPERSONAL PLANETS

are the outer planets.

♅ **Uranus:** cosmic consciousness, revolutionary change
♆ **Neptune:** spiritual awakening, cosmic love, all one
♇ **Pluto:** death and rebirth, deep, total change

ASTEROIDS

Between Mars and Jupiter, Asteroids reflect the awakening of feminine-defined energy centers in human consciousness.

Aspects included in this Wall Calendar are:

☉☌☽: Sun *conjunct* Moon means there is a Dark or New Moon.

☉☍☽: Sun *opposite* Moon means there is a Full Moon.

☉□☽: Sun *square* Moon means there is a Half Moon.

Ingresses (→): Indicate planets moving into new signs.

Sun Sign: The Sun enters a new sign once a month (around the 20th or so), completing the whole cycle of the zodiac in one year.

Moon Sign: The Moon changes signs approximately every $2^{1}/_{2}$ days, going through all twelve signs of the zodiac every $27^{1}/_{3}$ days (the sidereal month).

Moon Phases: are determined by the angle (aspects) between the Sun and the Moon.

D or R (Direct or Retrograde): Describes when a planet moves forward (D) through the zodiac or appears to move backward (R).

Lunar Rhythm

Everything that flows moves in rhythm with the Moon. She rules the water element on Earth. She pulls on the ocean's tides, the weather, female reproductive cycles and the life fluids in plants, animals and people. She influences the underground currents in earth energy, the mood swings of mind, body, behavior and emotion. The Moon is closer to the Earth than any other heavenly body. The Earth actually has two primary relationships in the universe: one with the Moon, who circles around her, and one with the Sun, whom she circles around. Both are equal in her eyes. The phases of the Moon reflect the dance of all three: the Moon, the Sun and the Earth, that together weave the web of light and dark into our lives. No wonder so much of our life on Earth is intimately connected with the phases of the Moon!

For each of the eight Moon phases (depicted in the outer rim of the chart to the right), the angle between the Sun and Moon (as reflected to Earth) progresses by 45-degree increments. Each lasts approximately 3–4 days of the Moon's entire 29½ day cycle.

Musawa © Mother Tongue Ink 2004

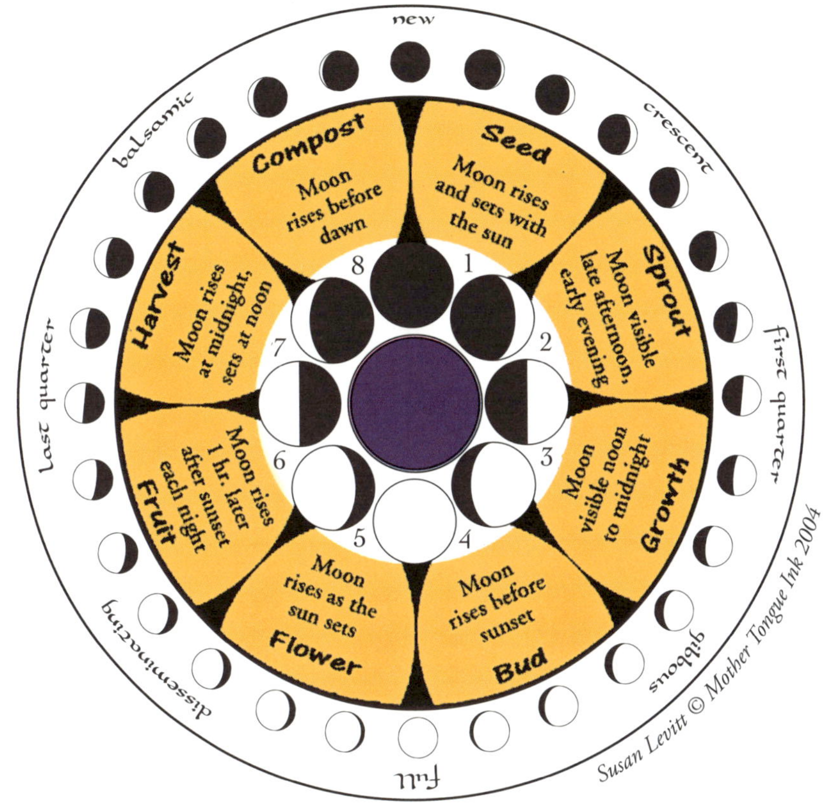

Susan Levitt © Mother Tongue Ink 2004

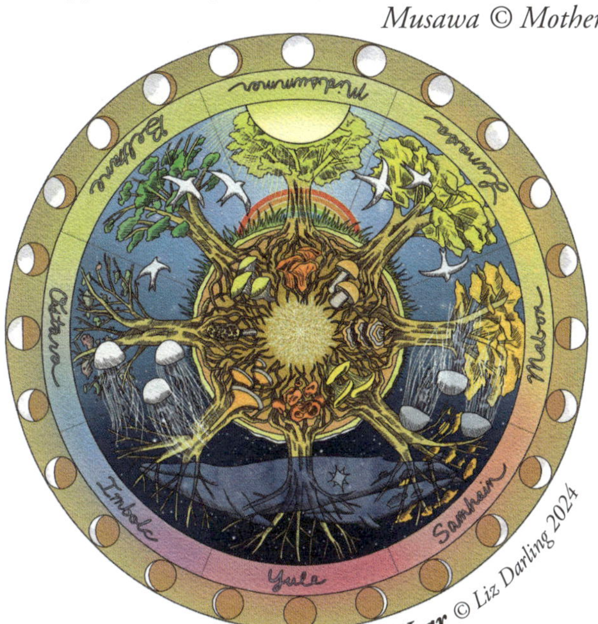

Wheel of the Year © Liz Darling 2024

Introduction to the Holy Days

At twelve, confronted with the absurdities and moral contortions of christian doctrine, I declared myself an atheist. It felt like a clean break, but doctrine has a long half-life. I spent decades unlearning what had been embedded—especially around holidays, where obligation, guilt, and enforced cheer lingered most stubbornly. Christmas, in particular, felt less like celebration than compliance.

In college, we formed an atheist organization to counter the aggressive christian movements on campus. Their slogan was ONE WAY. Ours was NO WAY. It was oppositional, necessary at the time, but still reactive. What I hadn't yet learned was that refusal alone leaves an emptiness longing to be filled.

Researching the origins of christian holidays cracked something open. I learned how thoroughly they had been appropriated from older, earth-based traditions—seasonal rites rooted in land, labor, and survival. Instead of christmas, we celebrated Saturnalia, the Roman winter festival of reversal and release: roles inverted, boundaries loosened, bodies fed and adorned. It was playful, unruly, and deeply human.

A few years ago, I began writing seasonal pagan holiday letters to friends. It was part reclamation, part invention: a way to refuse inherited rituals that no longer fit, while reviving and reshaping older ones. I wanted to mark the turning of the seasons, to remember holidays that honored darkness as well as light, decay as well as growth.

The pagan Wheel of the Year gave me a map—not linear, but cyclical—for living inside change. I think, now, I'd call myself an animist: from *anima*, breath, spirit, life. The understanding, shared by Indigenous peoples across the world, that all things are alive and ensouled—stones, storms, seeds, stories.

Rather than the christian mandate to dominate and conquer nature, animism invites relationship. We are not above the world, nor separate from it. We are embedded, entangled, and accountable—breathing with the land, listening for what it asks of us, now.

Molly Martin © Mother Tongue Ink 2026

The Wheel of the Year: Holy Days

The seasonal cycle of the year is created by the Earth's annual orbit around the Sun. Solstices are the extreme points as Earth's axis tilts toward or away from the Sun—when days and nights are longest or shortest. On equinoxes, days and nights are equal in all parts of the world. Four cross-quarter days roughly mark the midpoints in between solstices and equinoxes. We commemorate these natural turning points in the Earth's cycle. Seasonal celebrations of most cultures cluster around these same natural turning points:

February 2, Imbolc/Mid-Winter: celebration, prophecy, purification, initiation—Candlemas (Christian), New Year (Tibetan, Chinese, Iroquois), Tu Bi-Shevat (Jewish). Goddess Festivals: Brighid (Celtic), Yemanja (Brazilian).

March 20, Equinox/Spring: rebirth, fertility, eggs—Passover (Jewish), Easter (Christian), Norooz/New Years Day (Persian). Goddess Festivals: Eostare, Ostara, Oestre (German), Astarte (Semite), Persephone (Greek), Flora (Roman).

May 1, Beltane/Mid-Spring: planting, fertility, sexuality—May Day (Euro-American), Walpurgisnacht/Valborg (German and Scandinavian), Root Festival (Yakama), Ching Ming (Chinese), Whitsuntide (Dutch). Goddess Festivals: Aphrodite (Greek), Venus (Roman), Lada (Slavic).

June 21, Solstice/Summer: sun, fire festivals—Niman Kachina (Hopi), Tirgan (Persian). Goddess Festivals: Isis (Egyptian), Litha (N. African), Yellow Corn Mother (Taino), Ishtar (Babylonian), Hestia (Greek), Sunna (Norse).

August 2, Lammas/Mid-Summer: first harvest, breaking bread, abundance—Green Corn Ceremony (Creek), Sundance (Lakota). Goddess Festivals: Corn Mother (Hopi), Amaterasu (Japanese), Hatshepsut's Day (Egyptian), Ziva (Ukraine), Habondia (Celtic).

September 22, Equinox/Fall: gather and store, ripeness—Mabon (Euro-American), Mehregan (Persian), Sukkoth (Jewish). Goddess Festivals: Tari Pennu (Bengali), Old Woman Who Never Dies (Mandan), Chicomecoatl (Aztec), Black Bean Mother (Taino), Epona (Roman), Demeter (Greek).

October 31, Samhain/Mid-Fall: underworld journey, ancestor spirits—Hallowmas/Halloween (Euro-American), Dia de Muertos (Mexico), All Souls Day (Christian). Goddess Festivals: Baba Yaga (Russia), Inanna (Sumer), Hecate (Greek).

December 21, Solstice/Winter: returning of the light—Kwanzaa (African-American), Soyal (Hopi), Jul (Scandinavian), Cassave/Dreaming (Taino), Chanukah (Jewish), Christmas (Christian), Festival of Hummingbirds (Quecha), Shabeh Yalda/Birth Night (Persian), Koliada (Slavic). Goddess Festivals: Freya (Norse), Lucia (Italy, Sweden), Sarasvati (India).

* Note: Traditional pagan Celtic / Northern European, Jewish and Muslim holy days start earlier than the customary Native / North American ones—they are seen to begin in the embryonic dark phase: e.g., at sunset, the night before the holy day—and the seasons are seen to start on the Cross Quarter days before the Solstices and Equinoxes. In North America, these cardinal points on the wheel of the year are seen to initiate the beginning of each season.

© Mother Tongue Ink 2003

Borrowed from these sources with perm[illegible]sion:
The Grandmother [illegible] Time
by Z. Budap[illegible] 1989;
Celestially Auspicious [illegible]casions
by Donna Hen[illegible] 1996; &
Songs of Bleeding *by [illegible]ider, 1992*

Holy Days for 2027

Imbolc (February 2)

Have you heard of the Persephone Period? It's a concept many gardeners are just discovering, and it's proving to be a surprisingly useful guide.

Most of us know the myth of Persephone, daughter of Zeus and Demeter, the goddess of agriculture. Abducted by Hades and taken to the underworld, Persephone's absence plunged Demeter into grief, causing the earth to go barren. A compromise was eventually struck: Persephone would spend part of each year below ground, bringing winter, and return each spring to restore fertility and growth.

The Persephone Period describes a universal threshold when diminishing daylight signals plants to slow or stop growth, conserving energy through dormancy until light and warmth return—a rhythm gardeners can honor by timing planting to the sun rather than the calendar.

In gardening terms, the Persephone Period begins when day length drops below ten hours and ends when it rises above that threshold again. Across much of the Northern Hemisphere, this usually spans mid-November to early February, beginning around Samhain and ending near Imbolc.

In our garden, this is a quiet, hopeful time. Early flowers bloom. We pull weeds easily from damp soil and plan for the coming season. We welcome the gradual return of the light, tend our inner gardens, and gather with friends to cultivate warmth, rest, and enduring connections.

Spring Equinox / Ostara (March 20)

One sunny Spring day recovering from back surgery, finally able to walk around and sit outside, I spent an hour or so just watching pollinators. The air was full of flying and floating things. Filaments of spider web, falling blossoms, puffs of seeds and insects moved through the air in the soft breeze. Honeybees populated the orange and apple trees while the native bees stayed loyal to the native plants—everyone had their own niche! Our pollinator garden starts blooming early. The native carpenter bees and bumblebees especially love the red salvia. And there are all these other little pollinators that may or may not be bees, the kind that fly in squares turning quickly at right angles, the tiny gnats that circle endlessly around each other.

On the Spring Equinox we offer gratitude and honor all of the small beings that surround us. It's a time of renewal, of rejuvenation . . . scatter your own wildflower seeds of inspiration on the wind.

Beltane (May 1)

The Celts were a bunch of tree worshippers, and their pagan holiday of Beltane featured a May Bush, decorated and shown off around town. The Celts celebrated the holiday with big bonfires into which the May Bush was sacrificed in the grand finale. Beltane—May 1st—marks the Gaelic start of summer. Reason enough to cavort!

In this season we particularly appreciate our birds. One day I watched an elaborate dove mating ritual. There was wing flapping and feather ruffling and head bobbing and something that looked like passionate making out that involved grabbing each other's beaks and hanging on while dancing back and forth. This went on for quite a while. We saw these two lovebirds together several times in the weeks following their first dance. The couple, it turns out, only has to court once. They become a pair for the season.

Our Beltane celebration is fireless and smokeless and we don't decorate a May Bush, although we love the idea. But we do celebrate by appreciating the flora and fauna in our garden and neighborhood. Maybe we will take inspiration from the doves!

Summer Solstice (June 21)

Seeking rituals associated with solstices, I discovered one right here in the San Francisco Bay Area that has been ongoing since the 1960s: the quarterly circumambulation* of Mt. Tamalpais. (Tamalpais, so named by the native Coast Miwok people, was a sacred ceremonial site for the indigenous inhabitants of this land). I pledged to complete it for the summer solstice, and a sister hiker, Dolores, agreed to join me. At 89, Dolores was the oldest hiker, and I at 74 was was likely the second oldest.

Following the traditional clockwise direction, we performed Buddhist and Hindu chants, spells, sutras, and vows at natural features along the way. At our second station, led by an Iranian-American woman, we circumambulated a serpentine cairn, each tossing a stone upon it and chanting *Zan, Zendigi, Azadi. Women, Life, Freedom.* The spark for this chant and an uprising of Iranian women was the death of Mahsa Amini, a young Kurdish woman who died after being detained by Iran's morality police for "improper hijab."

For me this was the highlight of our trip. I was delighted to be led in this chant, in solidarity with Iranian women who have been risking their lives to protest for women's rights and equality.

Circumnavigate that which you wish to amplify this Summer Solstice.

**Circumambulation, or* pradakśinā *in Sanskrit, is the act of moving around a sacred object. It is an integral componant of Hindu and Buddhist devotional rituals. It's also present in Christian, Judaic, and Islamic practices.*

Lammas (August 2)

At Summer Solstice I celebrate my mother's birth day. On August 9, I mark her death day, which is also Nagasaki day, the day in 1945 when we, the Americans, dropped the atomic bomb on Nagasaki, Japan. August 6 was Hiroshima.

People all over the world mark the anniversary of the nuclear bombings. Some people fast from August 6 to 9, a nonviolent tradition to pause, reflect and create empathy for those who have suffered from nuclear weapons. Others fold 1,000 origami cranes, a long tradition in Japan, believed to bring a peaceful and healthy life. After the nuclear bombing, origami crane folding became an action for peace and nuclear abolition. It started in response to the story of Sadako Sasaki, a child who contracted leukemia from the radioactive fallout. She tried to make 1,000 cranes but died before she could finish. Her classmates finished the 1,000 cranes, making crane folding their message for peace, now an international tradition.

This Lammas season, think about what harvest of healing and hope you would like to share with your community, or that you can join. Maybe fold some origami cranes with friends in peaceful solidarity.

Fall Equinox / Mabon (September 22)

It felt like fate. On our very first date, a hike in the hills above Muir Beach, Holly and I bonded over plants. She pointed out a lichen growing on an oak tree—usnea. *To identify it,* she said, *you snap a branch and pull it apart until you see the central cord inside.*

A sensitive bioindicator of air quality, usnea only thrives where the air is clean and unpolluted. For centuries, it has been used in traditional medicine to treat wounds and infections. Today it's still valued—for easing sore throats, helping wounds heal, reducing fevers and pain, even as a possible cancer-fighting agent. Holly, now my wife, is a witch and an herbalist. She first learned about usnea from a teacher of medicinal plants, and today her garden overflows with remedies.

The Fall Equinox—Mabon—is our time to harvest herbs and brew up remedies. Holly stirs up her bite balm, a salve for every kind of skin irritation, while I turn to cannabis. Since I don't smoke, I've studied the alchemy of decarboxylation: gently heating the herb to unlock its powers before infusing it into oils for cooking. Together we blend teas from garden herbs.

Our garden is more than soil and stems. It is a living grimoire—a book of green magic—where medicine, ritual, and daily life are entwined. Harvesting and making are rituals of resistance too: an antidote to the anxiety of a world slipping toward authoritarianism. To touch leaf, fruit, and root is to salve our spirits, to root ourselves again in Mother Earth.

Samhain / Hallowmas (October 31)

The Cailleach looms across the landscape, creating mountains by flinging stones from her gigantic wicker basket. She is the crone goddess—ancient, white-haired and immense—whose footsteps shape the land itself. On Samhain, she takes command of the earth, ushering in winter and ruling until the thaw of spring. She governs storms, cold, and darkness, marking the moment when growth withdraws and survival becomes the central task.

Feared and revered for centuries, the Cailleach embodies winter's hard truths: scarcity, endurance, and the stripping away of what cannot last. "Winter is coming" is more than a seasonal warning; it names a recurring human condition, a time when resources tighten and tensions rise. Sometimes winter arrives quietly. Sometimes we realize, too late, that we are already inside it—politically, socially, or inwardly.

At Samhain, we stand at the threshold. We honor the Cailleach by gathering what we will need—strength, wisdom, community—to endure the inner and outer storms ahead.

Winter Solstice / Yule (December 21)

Years ago my wife Holly and I invented a Winter Solstice ritual we named *The Twelve Days of Solstice.* It starts on the Solstice, and ends with New Year's day, and involves making up our own daily rites and customs, observing the natural world and the changing of the seasons.

Our invention is aimed at supplanting the christian holiday. We are both ex-christians, she tortured by a more evangelical denomination than I by my pale protestant presbyterian sect. We still feel the need for tradition and ritual in our lives and so must invent our own.

We decorate a tree—a pagan custom we feel very good about reclaiming—taking all the time we like because why should we be in a hurry? One point of invention is to overcome all the obligations that make this holiday stressful, like holiday shopping—an unsustainable economic program that bankrupts the poor and does not fit well with our effort to consume less.

At Yule we seek to strengthen our community and mark the return of light. We gather with loved ones, shaping customs that keep us connected to one another and to the slow turning of the year. We invite friends to help us trim our Solstice tree, contribute to the local food bank, have neighbors over for hot chocolate, read poetry and stories aloud, bake edibles, host impromptu living room dance parties, cook savory soups, plant flower bulbs . . . With neighbors, we make signs and join street protests to raise our voices against fascism. We look for the sacred in everyday life.

Molly Martin

Amy Allen—Mandalamy Arts (Tacoma, WA) is a visual artist, homeschooling mom, and former clinical psychologist. She incorporates a sense of wonder, connection, inner healing, and empowerment into her art. FB, IG: @mandalamy_arts

Andria (Sacramento, CA) is a southern-born writer and poet. With deep ancestral roots in South Carolina, her work blends spiritual mysticism, historical memory, and the rhythms of nature.

Barbara Dickinson (Sunny Valley, OR) navigates life's winding paths with a heart full of wonder and a spirit ever open to adventure. With every step, she seeks wisdom, embraces change and challenge, and celebrates the fleeting beauty of each moment. May we all drink deeply from the well of inspiration and awe.

Bethroot Gwynn (Myrtle Creek, OR) 30 years as We'Moon's Special Editor and 50 at Fly Away Home women's land, growing food, theater and ritual. For info about spiritual gatherings, summertime visits, send SASE to POB 593, Myrtle Creek, OR 97457. For info about her book of poetry and plays, *PreacherWoman for the Goddess*.

Betty LaDuke (Ashland, OR) is an internationally renowned artist whose vibrant paintings celebrate the strength, dignity, and daily lives of women and communities around the world. Through decades of travel and cultural exchange, her work honors resilience, labor, and the sacred in ordinary life. bettyladuke.com

Carmen Sonnes (Salem, OR) creates paintings to bring beauty, healing and balance to our planet. By acknowledging culture, the feminine and spirit in each work, she fulfills her purpose. carmenrsonnes.com

Cat Lieser (Sitka, AK) finds inspiration paddling her kayak in secret ocean nooks.

Cathy McClelland (Kings Beach, CA) paints from her heart and imagination. Her inspiration comes from nature, cross-cultural mythical subjects, magical, sacred places and symbolism. It all fuels her creative soul. cathymcclelland.com, IG: @cathrynmcclelland

Cheryl Capaldo Traylor (Cary, NC) is a professional gardener and nature writer. She creates and tends beautiful gardens. Through writing she explores her lifelong love of nature and the mysteries of human life. cherylcapaldotraylor.com

Chris Cavan (Ontario, Canada) I am a grandmother, poet/writer, watercolour and mixed media artist who stays rooted to the sky among trees and by water. I create to delight, inspire and promote healing reflection. chris.cavan@rogers.com

Colleen Joy Corbe' Percival (Black Mountain, NC) I live in the Blue Ridge mountains—"Blue Smoke" by the Chereokee—in a one hundred year old house. My privilege to garden,walk near forested creeks, write and BE with my cat, dog, chickens and familia bring authentic beauty to me.

Deborah K. Snider (Silver City, NM) Deborah's career includes teaching art from kindergarten through college levels; arts administration, exhibitions curation, events management; overseeing diverse creative programs for communities and schools; and creating drawings, art quilts, and collages. debsniderart.com

Dorrie Joy (Somerset, UK) is an artist and craftswoman, poet, international speaker and ceremonial leader. She holds workshops as sacred spaces that centre creativity as an intentional practice of soul mending and belonging. Prints, originals, commissions, drums, love letters . . . dorriejoy.co.uk, IG: @dorrie.joy, FB: DorrieJoyArtist

Emily Kell (Boulder, CO) is a painter of feminine figures and faces. She honors the cosmic mother, the wild woman and all the women in between. All people who model for her work are friends, and they are fairly compensated for their contributions. emilykell.com, IG: @ emilythefunkypriestess

Gaia Orion (Ontario, Canada) is a successful international artist originally from Paris, France. She resides in the forest by a river. With her colorful symbolic art, she envisions a peaceful and flourishing world. gaiaorion.com, IG: @gaiaorionart

Heather Roan Robbins M.Th. (Ronan, MT) is a practical, intuitive, choice-oriented astrologer and author of *Starcodes-Choice-Based Astrology*, the *Starcodes AstroOracle Deck*, the *Wise Tree Oracle*, the weekly Starcodes astrological forecast, and the books *Starcodes, Moon Wisdom* and *Everyday Palmistry*. She organizes the Shining Mountains Grove for the Order of Bards, Ovates, and Druids, and has an on-line global practice. roanrobbins.com

Holly Wilkinson (Richmond, VT) is a listener and linguist, apprenticing herself to learn the languages and wisdom of milkweed, murmurations and the brook she has lived by for over 40 years. Catching wisps of poems in the wind is one of the joys of her way of living.

Jakki Moore (Co Leitrim, Ireland) lives with her two cats in an ancient Irish cottage, painting and writing. She does her best to grow her own herbs and vegetables and to live "off the land" with occasional forays to the shops for cat food and chocolate. jakkiart.com

Joanne M. Clarkson (Port Townsend, WA) is a palm and Tarot reader who also writes poetry. Her 6th collection, *Hospice House*, was published by MoonPath Press in 2023. Retired, she worked for many years as a Hospice Nurse. See more at joannethepsychic.com

Karen L. Culpepper (DC, Maryland, Virginia tri-state area) is a momma, creative, dreamer, herbalist and practitioner. She loves depth in her relationships, sunshine, being in saltwater, and laughter. Let's connect: IG: @rhythmicbotanicals, rhythmicbotanicals@gmail.com

Kirstin Litchfield (Gladstone, OR) is a writer and gardener.

Kitty Riordan (Alburquerque, NM) is a poet and visual artist who uses the creative process to continue the journey of staying wholehearted and present to self, earth and spirit. kittyriordan@hotmail.com

KT InfiniteArt (Freeport, NY) Creatrix, artist, writer inspired by sensuality and spirit. See IG: @KTInfiniteArt to check out more artwork. Prints and merchandise available: InfiniteArtWorld.com

Lillian Ruedrich (Gustavus, AK) is a digital photo artist, interpreting her images of the natural and wild world with filters and effects, finding the heart in each one to show the energy and magic shining through. scenesfromhome.com

Liz Darling (Pittsburg, KS) is a visual artist. With a meticulous approach and an emphasis on process and exploration, Liz creates symbolic imagery across media, examining the dissolution of boundaries between the body, nature, and the unseen. lizdarlingart.com, IG: @lizdarlingart

Lucy H. Pearce (Cork, Ireland) is the author of 12 non-fiction books: Nautilus winners *Medicine Woman, Burning Woman, Creatrix*, and Amazon #1 bestsellers *Crow Moon, She of the Sea,* and *Moon Time*. Founder of Womancraft Publishing and host of the Creative Magic podcast. lucyhpearce.com, IG: @lucyhpearce

Maria Silmon (North Yorkshire, UK) I love growth through learning. I create art based on what I am absorbed in, combining photography, painting, printing and craft. I am currently writing to aid the awakening of Starseeds. If interested please get in touch. mariasilmon.co.uk

Marla Faith (Nashville, TN) Inspired colorful uplifting mixed media collages, paintings, drawings, and fabric art at marlafaith.com, IG: @marla.faith

Marnie Recker (Tofino, BC) is a photographer and painter. My photographs are time capsules of people, place, love and light. I create paintings to honour the spirit of creativity and to celebrate the wondrous beauty in nature. marnierecker.com, IG: @marnieckerart, @marniereckerphoto

Megan Welti (St. Peter, MN) is an artist, poet and energy worker living in Western Massachusetts with her husband, four children, and many fur babies. IG: @redrootrising

Melissa Stratton Pandina (Westboro, MA) is an award winning painter. Her work centers on bringing folklore and stories to life. An illness led to her animism. She primarily works in oil and pen and ink and watercolor. deshria.com, IG:@deshriastudio

Molly Martin (Santa Rosa, CA) is a retired electrician whose focus for the past 50 years has been organizing for women's employment rights in the building trades and nontraditional work. Molly founded and edited the quarterly magazine *Tradeswomen*, and authored the books *Wonder Woman Electric to the Rescue* and *Hard-Hatted Women*. See more work at mollymartin.blog/author/tradeswomn, molly-martin.com. She also shares a travel blog with her wife Holly Holbrook: travelswithmoho.wordpress.com

Monisha Holmes (Fort Myers, FL) (she/her) is a multi-talented model and writer dedicated to promoting mental wellness and exploring spirituality for personal growth. With a Master of Science in Social Work from Columbia University, Monisha addresses the complex challenges of today's society. Her refreshing perspective on well-being can be found in publications like *Cosmopolitan Magazine, Teen Vogue, ShondaLand*, and *Bustle*. Informed by Humanistic Psychology, she inspires self-care and personal development through a magical lens. Monisha's dynamic background and commitment to holistic growth make her a powerful voice for authentic living.

Musawa (Estacada, OR and Tesuque, NM) Now in my 80s, I have been blessed to live in lesbian land communities for most of my adult life (We'Moon Land Community in OR, and ARF Womyn's Land in NM), and with my life partner, Eagle, since 1997. Coming up with the name "We'Moon" has been world-changing for me, throughout my own life cycle—and has inspired ever new generations of wemoon—as naturally as Mother Moon renews the creative life cycles of fertile womb-ones periodically, every moon month.

Niurka Guzmán Otañez (Cozumel, Mexico) is a Mexican artist of Dominican origin, has exposéd her work in France, Dominican Republic, Mexico, United States and Spain and has received numerous accolades in the disciplines of engraving, painting, and drawing, nationally and internationally. FB: niurkaguzmanotañez, IG: @ niurkaguzman

Patricia J Jensen (Moses Lake, WA) My goal is to use my artwork to visually influence the soul, the high-self, to understand and know itself at a deep level. Words sometimes are the least effective form of communication but artwork can stir intuition and knowledge that has been forgotten. IG: @art.patricia jensen, FB: Patricia Jensen

Patricia Rose (Seattle, WA) is a teacher, writer, traveler and mystic. She is answering a Call to be part of the movement that will restore the ancient power of sisterhood and return the sacred feminine to her rightful place. sherose.org and sherosewriting.substack.com

Sandra Pastorius (Ashland, OR) has been a practicing Astrologer since 1979, and a Featured Writer for We'Moon since 1990. Look for her collected We'Moon essays, "Galactic Musings" in the blogs at wemoon.ws. With Sun in Gemini, she delights in blending the playful and the profound. Sandra offers individual and couples charts, readings and transit updates in person or by phone. Email her about astrology classes at: sandrapastorius@gmail.com, and read more articles here: wemoon.ws/blogs/sandras-cosmic-trip. Peace Be!

Susan Levitt (San Francisco, CA) is an astrologer, tarot card reader and feng shui consultant since 1986. Her books include *Taoist Astrology* and *Introduction to Tarot*. She is also a chef who studies Chinese medicine and loves animals, especially birds. Follow Susan's lunar astrology newsletter for new Moon and full moon updates on her website. susanlevitt.com

Suzanne Grace Michell (Sacramento, CA) I am passionate about the interplay between the Divine, humanity, the natural world, and creativity. These connections inspire my life and art. It is a joy to share my work with you. RockMama.com

Tamara Phillips (British Columbia, Canada) is a watercolour artist inspired by the raw beauty of the natural world and our connection to it. She explores the depth between myth, dream, intuition, and reality. See more of her work at TamaraPhillips.ca, IG: @tamaraphillipsart

Tasha Zigerelli (Kamuela, HI) A ceremonialist, mother, writer, grief and death worker, Tasha weaves words on the portals of birth and death. Her first poetry book *The Blood of Roses* was published in 2024. She lives on Pele's alchemical land, Hawai'i island with her family. tendinggrief.com and @tashazigerelli

Tiffany Giasson (Poland, ME) draws inspiration from the beauty of nature and changing seasons. As a writer, artist, gardener, and visual creator, she channels her creativity into words and imagery that reflect her deep connection to Earth.IG: @toffeeleigh_

Trishna (New Delhi, India) FB, IG:@trishna777; Etsy: TrishnaPaints